Sir Seewoosagur Ramgoolam
Botanic Garden

JAMES DUNCAN
and the
GARDEN OF MAURITIUS

JAMES DUNCAN

and the

GARDEN OF MAURITIUS

ROBERT DUNCAN

Lurs Publishing
3 Blackie House, Lawnmarket, Edinburgh EH1 2NY
First published in 2007
Copyright © Robert Duncan 2007
ISBN 978-0-9555493-0-4
Made and printed in Great Britain by Syntax, Edinburgh

CONTENTS

PREFACE

James Duncan's name is frequently encountered in Mauritius, where the Botanic Garden at Pamplemousses is admired as an important national resource and there is interest in its history, but elsewhere it is another matter. Standard reference books have little to offer. Perhaps it is difficult to put him into categories. Director of a botanic garden, he was a gardener, not a botanist. A British gardener, he spent the most significant part of his life in the tropics. Head of one of the most famous of colonial botanic gardens whose work was closely linked to that of Sir William Hooker at Kew, he never received any formal training there. What I have attempted to do in this book is to gather together between one set of covers whatever firm – or at least probably firm – facts I could establish in order to throw some light on his life, character and achievements.

As a boy, I remember seeing a curiously shaped, dark brown object, hidden in the shadows of my grandfather George Duncan's rectory study, itself hardly changed from Victorian days. This must have been an example of the famed *Lodoicea maldivica*, the double coconut or coco de mer, found by early travellers floating in the sea, but eventually traced to the Seychelles in the Indian Ocean. Was it James Duncan who brought this object to Britain? It seems likely; and memories of it may have been what started me on this journey into the past.

There are two particularly important locations of letters written by James Duncan: the archives at the Royal Botanic Gardens, Kew, and the National Archives of Mauritius. Both sources are valuable, and both proved essential for the narrative which follows. However, these letters suffer from the same significant limitation. They are business letters, those to the government offices in Port Louis being mostly concerned with the administration and financing of the Botanic Garden at Pamplemousses and those to the director at Kew being concerned mainly with plant exchanges – though in the absence of more personal letters, these are the closest we now have to expressions of James Duncan's inner feelings. Fortunately, a man in his entirety did begin to emerge as I worked through the documents, and I hope that some of these pages will provide a more rounded impression of someone who had initially (for me) only the vaguest of outlines. There are still some major gaps in the record, particularly relating to James Duncan's early life and to the source(s) of his later prosperity. Perhaps this publication will bring other interesting documents to light.

One peculiarity in James Duncan's letters is the number of words spelt 'incorrectly' by modern standards. Some of them are simple errors, or represent a spelling which has changed in modern English, others seem to be a consistent idiosyncrasy on James's part. At least some of them are gardening terms which he must have seen frequently in reference books, for example, 'probigation' in place of 'propagation'. In any event, these eccentric spellings are part of his character, and I have not attempted to 'correct' them in any of the letters that follow, except for the scientific names of plants.

It is perhaps worth pointing out that a transcription is in any case a poor substitute for the original holograph, particularly regarding punctuation and the use of initial capital letters: there is an ambiguity in the written word which is not well served by the transcriber's need to come down on one side or the other, a full stop or a comma, a capital L or a lower case l. Parts of letters are impossible to decipher, particularly when James squeezes an extra line on to the already crowded sheet of the thin blue paper which he habitually used. But in general, his clear copperplate hand, with the old-fashioned double 's' (e.g. 'Pamplemoufses'), is easy to read.

A word on nomenclature. During its life of 250 years the Botanic Garden in Mauritius has been known by a range of names, from 'Le Jardin de Mon Plaisir', through 'Le Jardin du Roi' and 'The Royal Botanical Gardens, Pamplemousses' to the current 'Sir Seewoosagur Ramgoolam Botanic Garden', or 'SSR Botanic Garden' in abbreviation.

James Duncan used 'Royal Botanic Gardens' when he first arrived in Mauritius, but soon switched to 'Royal Botanical Gardens' to head his letters, though he used both forms freely in the body of letters. The official name at that time seems to have been 'Royal Botanical Garden', and that is what appears on the title page of James's *Catalogue of Plants*. To try to maintain consistency, when not quoting documents, I have used the form Royal Botanic Garden throughout, or the Garden for short.

The title of this book contains a deliberate ambiguity. The 'garden' that James came to know so well, was indeed the Botanic Garden. But Mauritius itself could be seen to be a garden in its own right. The story of changing attitudes to what grew on the island, the effects of the intervention of man, and the conflicts between what should have been done and what was actually done, form a background which I have touched on occasionally, relying heavily on some of the excellent books on the subject.

I owe thanks to many individuals and organisations whose time I have drawn upon. I am grateful to Library and Archives staff at the Royal Botanic Gardens, Kew, particularly Michelle Losse and James Kay, for providing access to letters and illustrations held in the archives, and to Gheeandut Suneechur and his colleagues at the National Archives, Mauritius for access to letters and other invaluable documents held there. I am also grateful for assistance from the Special Library and Archives, King's College, Aberdeen, the National Library of Scotland, Jane Hutcheon and her colleagues at the Royal Botanic Garden Edinburgh Library, Diane Mitchell at the National Museums of Scotland, Jane Hogan at Durham University Library, the National Archives, London, the British Library, the National Library of Mauritius, Tony Kanellos at the Library of Adelaide Botanic Garden, and Miguel Garcia at the Library of the Royal Botanic Gardens, Sydney. Julia Steele and Mark Nesbitt at the Economic Botany Collections, Kew, introduced me to actual plant specimens originally provided for Kew by James Duncan. Personal and family information has come from the Aberdeen and North-east Scotland Family History Society, the General Register Office for Scotland, Somerset Archive and Record Service, Somerset Register Office, Wiltshire and Swindon Record Office, and the National Record Office, Republic of Mauritius. Individuals who have been most kind in contributing their time and material evidence include Diane Baptie on matters of family history, Philip and Jean Day for the only surviving photographs of James Duncan, Anthony Duncan who lived on the island of Rodrigues when a child, John Duncan for his medals, Jim Endersby for sharing his wide knowledge of botanical history of this period, Bill Fraser, Ron Horne, editor of Ferdinand von Mueller's letters, Lord Howick and Robert Jamieson for the time spent showing me round and answering questions about the Howick Hall gardens, Sunil Ramkissoon for providing guidance on the streets of Port Louis, Guy Rouillard, to whom anyone who ventures to write on botanical matters in Mauritius owes a huge debt of gratitude, John and Annelyse Taylor, and Dominic Watt and Margaret Mackay, who each provided most helpful advice on the subject of James Duncan's peculiar spelling.

There are some other people to whom I owe a particular debt of thanks. Meghraj Aumeer, Officer in Charge of the SSR Botanic Garden, was most generous with his time and hospitality, providing me with guided tours of the Garden as it is today. Peter Duncan, maintainer of family records, acted as a sounding board as we endeavoured together to make sense of contradictions in the documents. Marina Carter, met by happy chance in the National Archives of Mauritius, guided me towards a number of obscure and valuable sources and has been very generous with her time and specialist knowledge. Henry Noltie first set me off on the right track of this story, put me straight on a large number of botanical issues, and has been kind enough to write the article on James Duncan's *Catalogue* which appears as an appendix to this narrative. (Errors and omissions which undoubtedly will be found in the book as a whole are, however, entirely my responsibility.) Finally, Jim McClure not only accompanied me on much of the travelling which resulted in the core of this book being written, but took most of the photographs for it, and proved to have an eagle eye for spotting crucial documents in a mass of apparently unrelated papers.

Some people may find the use throughout of the forename 'James' patronising, or on principle undesirable in a biography. It implies a lack of distancing by the biographer. I can only plead that it seems a reasonable form of address when writing of one's great great grandfather.

Robert Duncan
Edinburgh, 2007

1

PROLOGUE

If you walk in through the handsome, white painted iron gates of the main entrance to the Sir Seewoosagur Ramgoolam Botanic Garden of Mauritius (commonly referred to as Pamplemousses), you find yourself in a long straight avenue lined with closely planted, immensely tall palms and other tropical trees. This is Labourdonnais Avenue, named after the great French governor of the island which was called, in the eighteenth century, the Ile de France. Running parallel to this avenue, to the left, is the much more modest Duncan Avenue. Here, there are a few forest trees from different parts of the world, such as *Cinnamomum camphora*, from which camphor was obtained, and *Peltophorum pterocarpum*, the yellow flame tree from Australia, but the main planting consists of lines of crotons, shrubs with leaves striped yellow, green and brown, and a popular plant in today's garden centres. At the end of the path, the planting breaks up into a random assortment of spice trees and bushes: nutmeg, cinnamon, cloves, and allspice.

Crotons came originally from the Moluccas, part of today's Indonesia, and were studied and named by Dutch botanists in the 17th century. Carl Linnaeus (born just three hundred years ago) gave the plants their common name of croton in the 18th century and by the 19th century, they were already well known in Europe. The illustration opposite is a reproduction of a 19th century engraving based on a drawing by William Jackson Hooker, who at that time (1831) was Professor of Botany in Glasgow. He had been sent the plant from Mauritius by a naturalist named Charles Telfair. We will come across both Hooker and Telfair again later in this narrative.

Thirty years after the engraving was made, this particular species, *Codiaeum pictum*, was listed by James Duncan as one of several varieties of croton to be found in the Pamplemousses garden, when he came to prepare his *Catalogue of Plants in the Royal Botanical Garden, Mauritius*. James Duncan was director of the Garden from 1849 to 1865, and Duncan Avenue is named after him. When he arrived in Mauritius, there had already been a garden on the site for over a hundred years. The trees and shrubs which grow alongside the avenue today were planted very close to where a remarkable Frenchman named Pierre Poivre planted in 1770 spices acquired from the Moluccas, then controlled by the Dutch, in an attempt to win for France part of the lucrative spice trade. But by the time James Duncan arrived, the Garden was in a sorry state. His achievement, over fifteen years, was to rebuild it until it became the most popular place to visit on the island. He was effectively the founder of the Botanic Garden of Mauritius as we know it today.

This book is an account of James Duncan's life, in so far as it can be recovered, with, as background, a short account of how the Garden came into being. It is the story of a Victorian gardener from Scotland finding himself responsible for saving for future generations a beautiful tropical garden, perhaps the oldest tropical botanic garden that exists. In some ways, it is a typical tale: a number of other men from a similar background at that time followed similar careers far from home. But it is also a unique tale: an account of one individual with a strong character some of which comes across clearly more than 150 years later.

2

ILE DE FRANCE

Seen from the air, the bright green and pear-shaped island is surrounded by an almost continuous coral reef which has the appearance of white lace, irregularly following the outline of the land. The island measures 61 by 47 kilometres and lies 20° south of the equator, just within the Tropic of Capricorn, and so although tropical, it has distinct seasons, with an average summer temperature of 27° and an average winter temperature of 17°.

The volcanoes which originally led to the appearance of this land above the south Indian Ocean in the Pleistocene age are long extinct, unlike those of Réunion, lying 200 kilometres to the west and also part of the group known as the Mascarene Islands. There is a third significant island in the group, Rodrigues, which is now, and was throughout this narrative, politically part of Mauritius.

The Republic of Mauritius today has a population of over 1.24 million, which makes it one of the densest populated countries in the world, even though until four hundred years ago there were no human residents at all, and there were very few a mere three hundred years ago. The island's bright green colour today comes mainly from the sugar estates which cover most of the low lying land. At one time, the island was densely covered by forests, but many of these valuable trees were early victims of human occupation. Widespread erosion took place and the local climate changed. Mauritius subsequently became one of the first places in the world where the causes and results of soil erosion were understood: many of the ecological issues concerning the world today were first raised on this small tropical island in the eighteenth century.

The island is isolated, lying approximately 900 kilometres to the east of Madagascar and 4000 kilometres south-west of India. This isolation led to the development of an indigenous flora and fauna adapted to a specialised island habitat. Among the animals, giant tortoises and large flightless birds (including the dodo) were prominent. Not only were there no humans, the island was hardly inhabited by mammals, the only indigenous one being a fruit eating bat.

Arab traders sailing down the coast of Africa knew of the island, Austronesians from Borneo could have visited it on their long journey across the Indian Ocean to settle in Madagascar, and when Portuguese explorers rounded the Cape of Good Hope on their way towards India and the spice islands further east it was sighted by them. But it was the Dutch who eventually took possession of the island, in 1598, naming it Mauritius in honour of Prince Maurice of Nassau. No attempt to settle the island was made until 1638, but then, with the arrival of permanent inhabitants, the island started to undergo major ecological change.[1]

The initial damage was caused probably by rats, which would have reached land from ships wrecked off the coast. Subsequently, goats, pigs and dogs were introduced, all of which became feral. Finally, the new human settlers themselves found it all too easy to kill defenceless animals to extinction. It was the dodo that became the most potent emblem of change. Within a few decades it was extinct, leaving behind few traces except some skeletal remains and fame as the symbol of the destruction of species at the hands of modern man.

Plant life did not fare very much better. The main interest of the Dutch during their occupation was timber extraction, both for the home country itself, and for the Dutch colony on the Cape of Good Hope, whose own forests had been largely felled. The stands of mature ebony trees were cut down at such a rate in the course of the seventeenth century that concern was expressed even at that time.[2]

The settlement by the Dutch was never large and was hardly intended to be permanent, and in 1710 they finally abandoned the island. The island was not left empty for long – though empty is the wrong word, for the Dutch left behind them slaves who had been brought to the island from Africa and Madagascar and who had escaped. In 1715 the French, who already occupied the nearby island of Réunion (called Bourbon at that time), laid formal claim to Mauritius. Initially the island was governed by the French East India Company, the Compagnie des Indes. The Company wanted to forestall the British, who were eying the island as a possible staging post between St Helena and India. The French were also beginning to formulate a strategy intended to break the Dutch monopoly of the spice trade.

The first permanent settlements date from 1723. One of the first areas to be occupied was the well watered, flat plain to the north of the island known as 'Pamplemousses'. It is said that this word derives from 'pampel' meaning 'big' in Dutch and 'limoes' meaning 'lemon' in Malay. The use is first recorded in 1729 and perhaps the first French settlers found trees bearing fruit similar to grapefruits which had been imported by the Dutch from Amboyna, but no one really knows.[3] In any event, the area was colonised rapidly and in 1756 the Catholic church of St Francis was completed, the oldest on the island.

One of the most influential of the early governors of the Ile de France was Bertrand-François Mahé, Comte de La Bourdonnais, known today as Labourdonnais. He arrived on the island in 1735 and the following year acquired land in the Pamplemousses area. There he built a house and laid out a garden, the aim of the latter being to try out and acclimatise useful plants including subsistence crops, which were urgently needed by the growing population. The name of the property was Mon Plaisir.

One new crop was particularly successful, namely manioc, from which tapioca is derived and which, brought from Brazil, became a staple of the slave population. Maize, potatoes and rice were also grown, together with cotton and indigo. Labourdonnais did not remain long in the house itself: both his wife and son having died in 1738, he sold Mon Plaisir to the Compagnie des Indes, though he maintained his interest in the garden until he left the island in 1746.

Subsequent governors established their residence at Le Réduit, near Moka, where another botanical garden was established. The two gardens, Mon Plaisir and Le Réduit, were both used for experiments in planting. Apart from fruit and vegetables, mulberries were planted at Pamplemousses in an attempt to establish a silk industry, and in 1753 an apothecary botanist, recently arrived from Paris, began to collect medicinal plants for cultivation there. However, the most important purpose to which the garden was put was to serve as the base of a spice transplantation programme.

In 1764 the Compagnie des Indes transferred the Ile de France to the French Crown, and under the new form of government power was divided between a governor and an intendant, the former exercising military authority while the latter controlled finance and justice. The first intendant was to be Pierre Poivre, who already knew the island well. He was a naturalist who had travelled widely in Asia. For two years he had lived in Canton, where he developed an interest in both the aesthetics and the technologies of Chinese gardens. On his return journey to Europe, through a series of misadventures, he landed up in Java, where he acquired knowledge of both spice-tree culture in the Moluccas and the value to the Dutch of the monopoly trade in spices, particularly cloves and nutmeg. Poivre thought that the Ile de France would be the ideal place in which to establish a rival spice industry, and this became an overriding ambition for him. At the same time, he maintained his general interest in natural history, forestry and agriculture. In 1749 he visited Cape Town and was impressed by the Dutch Company Garden there. It was aesthetically attractive and at the same time set an example through its tree planting and acclimatisation practices. This influenced his later thinking both on the garden at Pamplemousses, which he was in due course to buy, and on the Ile de France itself, which he came to envisage as a garden in its own right.[4]

Poivre's first attempt to introduce a few nutmeg plants to the Ile de France was made in 1753 but was not successful.[5] He returned to France, where he became well known through writings and lectures on philosophical and agricultural matters, and in 1766 he was appointed *commissaire* of the Ile de France with the specific tasks of promoting the transfer of spices and of encouraging soil and forest conservation.

Soon after arriving back on the island, Poivre bought as his residence the house and garden of Mon Plaisir. He wrote, 'I have bought (on credit) from the Company a simple garden, ready-made and well watered, with the sole view of having somewhere ready and secure to put next March the plants that M. l'abbé Galloys will be sending me from China . . . I have bought the necessary slaves to cultivate the garden. I am having the land prepared specifically for this purpose, above all for the rare plants that I hope to obtain for this island, as well as for all the useful plants that I plan to gather from the different corners of Asia. I thought that the only way to succeed in this plan was to cultivate them at my expense, in my own way, under my eyes and on my own land, where I should be able to admit only those people whom I wanted.'[6]

In June 1770 two ships arrived in Port Louis harbour carrying the precious spices – a large number of nutmeg seeds and seedlings and a smaller quantity of clove seedlings. They were identified by the eminent naturalist Philibert Commerson, another distinguished scientist by then living on the island, and planted in the gardens of Mon Plaisir. Poivre kept the plants under his direct control, and it was during this period that the serious history of the Pamplemousses garden as a botanic garden began. Other useful plants introduced by him included varieties of wheat, rice, and grasses, indigo, tea, fruit trees, and resin and oil producing trees. Ornamental plants included hibiscuses, roses, orchids, and water-lilies. It is notable that many of these plants were drawn widely from Asia and Africa, and not, as often happened in such colonial situations, from the home country.

Poivre finally left the island in 1772, as a result of political manoeuvring in both the Ile de France and Paris, and the land was bought by the Government. Subsequently it was divided into several sections. One part, which included the house, retained the name Mon Plaisir; another part was named Le Jardin du Roi. Before leaving the Ile de France, Poivre had arranged that direction of the garden should be carried on by a young Creole, named Jean Nicolas de Céré. Son of a naval officer, Céré had been born on the Ile de France in 1737 and Poivre remained in touch with him through a lengthy correspondence which continued up to his death in Lyon in 1786.

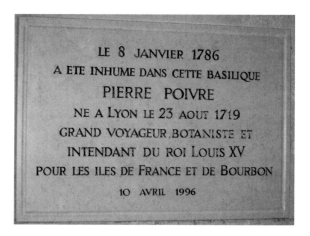

LE 8 JANVIER 1786
A ETE INHUME DANS CETTE BASILIQUE
PIERRE POIVRE
NE A LYON LE 23 AOUT 1719
GRAND VOYAGEUR BOTANISTE ET
INTENDANT DU ROI LOUIS XV
POUR LES ILES DE FRANCE ET DE BOURBON
10 AVRIL 1996

Céré took on his task with enthusiasm, even though he had no professional training. 'I have been compelled to become a kind of botanist,' he wrote.[7] He tended the young spice plants with care and the first cloves were picked in October 1776 in the presence of the governor and the intendant, to be sent to the king. The nutmeg plants were more difficult, but in due course they too were fruitful. Even though the climate of the Ile de France turned out eventually not to be suitable for the commercial cultivation of these spices, the Jardin du Roi became the nursery where plants were reared and the research centre from which scientific knowledge of their culture spread. It is likely that the clove trees that eventually brought such prosperity to Zanzibar were descended from plants developed on Mauritius.

Céré developed a correspondence on the subject of tropical plants with botanists in many countries, leading to the Jardin du Roi being ranked among the most famous gardens of the time. A visitor in 1786 described the Garden as 'one of the marvels of the world'. Indeed, Richard Grove points out that by the end of the 18th century, the Ile de France as a whole occupied a far more significant place in French philosophical, scientific and even literary thinking than was ever the case with the island colonies of other European powers like Britain or the Netherlands.[8]

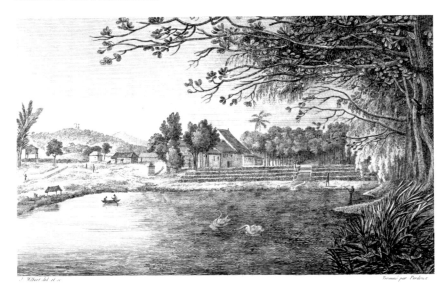

I should mention one other contributor to the fame of the Ile de France at that time, namely Jacques-Henri Bernardin de St Pierre. He was an engineer by training and arrived on the island in July 1768, in other words, soon after Pierre Poivre, who quickly became his mentor on matters environmental and moral (both men were opposed to slavery in principle, which did not stop them employing slaves in practice.) Bernardin remained on the island for only two years, but these marked the rest of his life. Observant by nature, he took notes of all he saw and in 1773, following his return to France, he published his *Voyage à l'Isle de France* which attracted immediate attention – the book was published in English in 1775, and Bernardin became a friend of Jean-Jacques Rousseau. It remains a superb and very readable account of the island at that time. However, Bernardin's real fame (and fortune) were made by his publication in 1787 of *Paul et Virginie*, a tragic romance based on real events and given a real location which encouraged readings of the book both as an early and influential example of romantic fiction, and as a slice of real history; the latter leading to curiosities like the 'tomb' of the doomed lovers which can still be visited today in the Garden at Pamplemousses.

3

A BRITISH COLONY

In 1810, the Ile de France passed from French to British hands, an acquisition which was ratified by the treaties marking the end of the Napoleonic wars.

War had continued on and off between the two countries for a hundred years, fought by land and more particularly by sea in the Americas, Africa and Asia, as well as in Europe. The Ile de France, along with the other French owned Mascarene Islands of Bourbon and Rodrigues, lay on the main British shipping route between India and Europe via the Cape, and French corsairs based in the Ile de France made substantial profits by capturing British merchant ships during the early years of the 19th century. Britain decided that action was needed to protect her commerce.

Following several inconclusive skirmishes, a decision was taken to invade the islands. In 1809 troops occupied Rodrigues, and used it as a base from which to capture Réunion, whose name had been changed from Bourbon by the Convention in Paris in 1793. The campaign for the Ile de France started badly for the British, whose ships suffered a humiliating defeat at the battle of Grand Port – this defeat for the British is said to be the only French naval victory recorded on the Arc de Triomphe in Paris. But it did not delay the inevitable result for long. The action was re-created by Patrick O'Brian in fictional terms, but based on historical fact, in his novel *Mauritius Command*.

> The conquest of Mauritius ran its leisurely course, with the regiments marching and countermarching in a scientific manner that pleased the generals on either side. The infantrymen sweated, but few of them bled. They had been landed smoothly, without opposition, and they presented General Decaen with an insuperable problem. His numerous militia was no use to him at all: most of its members . . . had already seen copies of General Farquhar's proposed proclamation, all of them were more concerned with the revival of their strangled trade than with the welfare of Buonaparte's

empire. His Irish troops were clearly disaffected; his French regulars were outnumbered by well over five to one; and his navy was blockaded by an overwhelming force of ships. His only concern was to delay General Abercrombie's advance until his surrender should meet certain arcane military requirements, so that he should be able to justify his conduct at home and obtain honourable terms at Port-Louis for himself and his men. He succeeded to admiration.[1]

The terms of the surrender were generous. The new British governor, Sir Robert Farquhar, took over the administration of the colony (which reverted to its former name of Mauritius) in a manner that was sympathetic to the inhabitants. The French were guaranteed their property, their language, and their laws – their way of life. British appointments were made to a few key positions, but most retained their French incumbents. One of these was the post of director of the Jardin du Roi.

However, Nicolas Céré had died that same year of 1810 after many decades spent enhancing the Garden's reputation, and his place as director was taken by his son, Auguste. The son appears not to have been equal in talents to the father, and a confusing period for the Garden now began. Major-General Ralph Darling, who commanded the troops in Mauritius from 1818, and who on occasion stood in as acting governor, described Auguste Céré as 'a man of indolent habit, appearing from the present state of the garden, to possess neither science, activity of body or energy of mind'.[2] It was decided to split management responsibilities in the Garden. Auguste Céré remained in a subordinate role until he retired in 1823, but Dr William Burke, government chief medical officer, was brought in as superintendent.

Burke, not surprisingly, laid emphasis on the development of plants with medical properties, and is recorded as having been responsible for introducing *Alstonia scholaris*, whose bark is used in traditional medicine for bowel complaints, *Gloriosa superba*, which is extremely poisonous but was used in traditional medicine for a wide range of ailments, and *Vitis quadrangularis*, which contains calcium, carotene and ascorbic acid, and is known as the 'bone setter'.[3] In spite of Dr Burke's efforts, however, the Garden was in decline.

In 1820 a new director, John White, was appointed. General Darling wrote of him: 'It is now in charge of a Mr White who had the superintendence on a former occasion and, as he has the merit of assiduity and is not totally unskilled, the garden even in his hands may be expected to improve, though it can never become what was originally intended, or what it could be capable of under a competent person.'[4]

Darling himself cannot have helped matters. The old house of Mon Plaisir had already been detached from the garden and now it was rebuilt. When completed, he moved into it as his residence and he seems to have treated the Botanic Garden as his own private grounds. This new Mon Plaisir is basically the handsome colonial style building which is still to be seen, though it was considerably modified at some point after 1839 and was not made part of the Botanic Garden again until 1878. Today it is the administrative centre of the Garden.

Dr Burke left the colony in 1825 and the following year John White was replaced as well. Responsibility for the Garden remained divided between a director and a superintendent. Charles Telfair, the surgeon and experienced naturalist who was to send the croton to Glasgow, was appointed superintendent. For the post of director, the London minister responsible, Lord Bathurst, sent out from Britain a certain John Newman.

For a time, things may have gone well. A visitor to the island in 1829 was Elizabeth Grant, author of the *Memoirs of a Highland Lady*, on her way back to Britain from India with her new Irish soldier husband. She included her impressions of Mauritius in her book.

At length on Xmas morning we came in sight of the Isle of France, and before dinner time we were at anchor in the harbour at port Louis. It was a pretty scene, plenty of shipping on the sea, plenty of wood on the shore, hills in the distance, and a long straggling town lying along the water's edge. . . .

We enjoyed this month extremely. It was hot sometimes at night in the town, but the breeze which came up with the tide always, refreshed the air again and the house was large and roomy, standing back from the street in a courtyard of good size, and with corridors running thro' it, which kept it as cool as could be managed without Verandahs, which luxury and ornament cannot be indulged in here on account of the hurricanes. No year passes without two or three of these destructive storms. The winds are so big, so eccentrick is their course, so overpowering that they sweep off a great deal of property, in spite of every precaution. All buildings are low, there are no projections, nothing that can be caught at, and yet no place quite escapes damage at one time or another.

The scenery is more pretty and quiet and interesting than fine. A plain of fertility beyond the town, bordered by the sea and rising to the mountains, which are some of them picturesquely peaked. 'Peter Botte' very conspicuous. The nutmeg wood belonging to the Government, and beautifully kept, is one of the most interesting spots to drive thro' from the beauty of the trees; large, tall, forest trees, they are full of branches and dark leaves, so very fragrant, and the spice in all its stages bursting all around. The nutmeg, quite red when growing, peeps out from its covering of green mace, quite like a flower. The Cinnamon bushes were the underwood, their buds — the cassia buds of commerce — scenting the air.[5]

I cannot say for sure that this spice wood was the garden at Pamplemousses, but if it was, it would seem that in 1830, at least, Poivre and Céré's spice plantation was being well maintained. Charles Telfair was said to have 'stimulated Newman to activity; he rescued the Garden to a certain extent from its derelict condition, adding some new species, and replacing others which had been destroyed.' However, he allowed himself to be distracted from his public work by devoting much time and care to his own property, 'Bois Cheri', and in 1829 the post of superintendent was abolished.[6]

From that date Newman was on his own. Perhaps Telfair was glad to be rid of him. In a letter to Sir William Hooker of 1832 he wrote that Newman had 'many good qualities but a jealousy of amateurs and a kind of bristling noli me tangere feeling in his profession render him rather difficult to deal with.'

Newman himself described his new responsibility in this way. 'The garden, although laid out in the oldest French style, has the advantage of being irrigated, thereby saving a number of hands.' He proceeded to divert some of the irrigation and some of the spare hands to his own private use. He obtained from the government a concession of part of the land in order to form an 'experimental garden' where young workers could be trained as gardeners, in order to carry their acquired skills to other parts of the island. However, the original purpose of this concession was quickly forgotten and Newman, as proprietor of the land, exploited the available labour to his own profit, growing vegetables and pineapples. He also managed to change the course of a canal, diverting on to his own land water that should have been available to the public garden.

In 1838 a visitor to the Garden reported that trees were dying of old age, avenues were blocked, and whole areas had been abandoned. No one seemed to be working there. The governor, Sir Lionel Smith, after being taken on a tour, asked his guides: 'But pray, where is the cultivated part?' The reply was simple – he had seen everything.

The situation had become so shocking that the governor did eventually request a report. The conclusion, delivered in 1844, read:

The whole is in such a deplorable state of neglect and abandonment that the Committee rather than see things continue in the same state would not hesitate to recommend that the establishment should no longer be kept up.

But however painful it may be to the Committee, they feel it their duty in order to attain the object in mind, to recommend the removal of M. Newman as director of the Botanical Gardens, except if he immediately and honestly adopts a different course.[7]

But Newman was to remain in his post until he died, in 1848, after over twenty years as director. Towards the end of his life, the government made a request that he should at least live in his house which adjoined the Garden. His reply to the colonial secretary was that he had let the house to a Dr Reilly, but that he had now given him notice, and therefore requested 40 dollars a month rent as compensation. Alternatively, the government would have to buy the house.[8] Which is what happened.

By this time, enough information about the state of affairs had reached London to ensure that action would have to be taken. For the time being, on Newman's death, an acting director was appointed. This was Dr Wenceslas Bojer, an eminent botanist of Czech origin who had known Mauritius since 1821. He had been a founder member, with Telfair and others, of the Société d'Histoire Naturelle, which later became the Royal Society of Arts and Sciences, and he had published in 1837 *Hortus Mauritianus*, a catalogue of over 2,000 species of plants found in Mauritius.[9]

Bojer described the Garden as being in a state of wilderness, 'overgrown with useless plants, weeds and destructive creepers.' 60 men would be needed for 18 months to get it all sorted out. Otherwise, 'it would be far preferable to abandon the Gardens altogether.'[10]

However, Bojer seems to have had personal ambitions of his own, and may have wanted to take over the land for commercial speculation. Perhaps it was because of this that he turned out to be not entirely helpful to the new director, when the latter arrived.

For London had now taken up the case. The secretary of state for the colonies, Earl Grey, exercised his powers of appointment and patronage and named his own head gardener to be the next director of the Royal Botanic Garden in Mauritius. In the summer of 1849, therefore, James Duncan and his family set sail for the island.

4

James Duncan – the early years

According to his gravestone, a piece of pink Aberdeenshire granite, set down somewhat incongruously among the limestone slabs of a Cotswold churchyard, James Duncan was born 'near Aberdeen in October 1802'. Exact details of his origins are as difficult to discover as this uncertainty implies. It is possible that the stone was not in fact erected at the time of his death. His widow Sarah, who survived him by nearly twenty years, is recorded as being 'interred here', but for James, the inscription on the stone says only, 'In affectionate remembrance of James Duncan for many years director of the Botanical Gardens Mauritius'. The stone was perhaps erected following Sarah's own death, in 1894.

We do not know exactly where he was born. One possibility is the town of Banchory, 25 kilometres west of Aberdeen up the Dee road, where, according to family tradition, his ancestors had been crofters.[1] His grandmother Jane Duncan, who died in 1841, was certainly buried there. Her grave was visited on 18th October that year by his uncle John, the family poet, who recorded the visit as follows:

> From where the city spires uprear,
> And scenes of life abound,
> A stranger I, a pilgrim here,
> Now tread on kindred ground.
>
> The recent wound still pains my heart
> Still warmly falls the tear;
> Cold duty claim'd the solemn part,
> Lately performed here.
>
> I late consign'd my dearest friend,
> To this unwelcome cave;
> Pale grief's *sad recollections* blend,
> To mourn beside her grave.[2]

Perhaps not surprisingly, John the Poet died penniless in Aberdeen in 1850, and was buried at the expense of his elder brother William, James's father.

No record of the date when James was born has been found, either, and indeed, many years later, he was unable to provide evidence of his age when the time came to negotiate his pension. 'Mr Duncan states,' Mr Cardwell at the Colonial Office wrote to the governor of Mauritius, 'that he is upwards of sixty years of age, though he is unable to procure any evidence on that point.' Perhaps he was born in October 1802 as his gravestone says, perhaps not.

Similarly, there seems to be no surviving documentary information about his mother, although her name is supposed to have been Mary Reid. Were his parents married? When was Mary born and when did she die? We don't know. However, in 1810, by which time James was perhaps aged seven, there is evidence of his father's marriage to Margaret Shepherd. This wedding took place on 16th June, when William was about thirty, and his wife a little older. They were married in Old Machar, Aberdeen, possibly in the cathedral church of St Machar. There is no record of any children, until the birth of a daughter, Helen Jean, on 14th November 1823, and her baptism on the same day. (She was later known as Helen Jane.) These events took place in the parish of Fetteresso, to the south of Aberdeen, in Kincardineshire. The entry in the parish record states that the father, William Duncan, was a farmer from Newtonhill and that the witnesses were James Duncan and Margaret Milne.

Newtonhill is today a commuter town for Aberdeen, but in those days it was a small Kincardineshire village perched on cliffs of mica schist above the bay where the Burn of Elsick runs into the North Sea. Fishing boats would have pulled up on this sheltered shore and even now fields run right to the edge of the cliff. It is possible that the family's home was Newtonhill Farm itself, whose house (now unoccupied) stands on the crest of a hill with views down to the old village and Newtonhill Bay. By 1823, the mediaeval parish church of Fetteresso, outside Stonehaven, had been abandoned for a new church in the centre of the town. However, there was another church close to Newtonhill at Cammachmore, and perhaps that is where Helen Jean was baptised.

It is interesting that one of the witnesses at the baptism was William's son James. According to the traditional family account, James left home early because he could not get on with his stepmother. If, however, he was present at the baptism of his stepsister when he was already aged 21, the traditional account may not be correct, and he may have spent most of his youth near Newtonhill, where the surrounding hamlets have names which superbly evoke the landscape: Windyedge, Stoneyhill, Harecraig, Quoscies, Beltcraig, and Aquhorthies.

This is rolling farmland of dry stone walls enclosing fields of corn and pasture for cattle. It had then a strongly individual character. The farms in those days were small and literacy levels were high. This was perhaps the area of Scotland where the tradition of a school in every parish was strongest and many teachers were graduates of one of Aberdeen's two universities. But there was also a need for labour on the farms, and if it was the case that James Duncan had few, if any, male siblings, the farm rather than the school might have had first claim on his time.

The population of the city of Aberdeen expanded greatly in the early nineteenth century, rising from about 27,000 in 1801 to 72,000 by 1851, largely reflecting the boom in the textile industry. This growth led to an increased demand for milk and vegetables, and by 1831 William Duncan was listed in the Aberdeen Post Office Directory as a gardener in Berryhill. In 1835 he was living at 50 John Street, and by 1840 he had moved into the probably newly built Millbank Cottage in Berryden, located in the area between Old Aberdeen and the new city.

This district was outside the built up part of the city, and was devoted to market gardens. William was by then, if he had not been before, a market gardener, for the Post Office Directory listed, in addition to his house, a stall at the new market, which had recently been built between Union Street and the harbour.

Millbank Cottage still exists, hidden behind a high fence, and raised on a plateau containing not only the solidly built granite cottage but also a front garden. In William's time, there would have been fine views south over the expanding city of Aberdeen, but today the distant views are blocked by high buildings and inner suburban businesses. The house consists of four well proportioned rooms on the ground floor, with a curving stair leading up to bedrooms on the upper floor. Most of the stone fireplaces have survived.

One can only speculate about James's education, and even about his early training as a gardener. Perhaps, like Joseph Paxton, who was an almost exact contemporary and who came from a similar (but English) background, James worked first on a local aristocratic estate, such as Crathes, and went on to work as a trainee at one of the major training gardens of the early 19th century. The Royal Botanic Garden Edinburgh would have been one such possibility, but no relevant records survive. Paxton himself went to London to enter the garden of the Horticultural Society, whose *Handwriting Book of Under Gardeners and Labourers* contains Paxton's entry in 1823. Hoping to find something similar, I visited the RHS library and turning a page was thrilled to find a copper plate entry for James Duncan in March 1827. But it was a different one. This James Duncan was born in Perthshire in 1805 and worked at the Earl of Mansfield's garden at Scone before travelling to London.[3]

Another possibility is that 'our' James Duncan trained at Kew, but this is unlikely given that there is no evidence of early familiarity with the garden in his extensive correspondence with Sir William Hooker. Moreover, he shows no sign of acquaintanceship with John Smith, another Scottish gardener, who, following four years in the Edinburgh garden, went south to Kew in 1822 and was curator there from 1842 to 1864, being a recipient of some of James's letters from Mauritius. It is of course possible that he had little formal education and that his eccentric spelling is an indication of this. But if that was the case it is hard to explain how an ill-educated farmer's son from Aberdeenshire turned up in a not unimportant job in Somerset, just about as far from Aberdeenshire as one can go within Britain.

For it is at this point, in 1835, that the story becomes clearer. James, by then aged 32, on 20th January married Sarah Biggs, at St James's church, Paddington, in London. Sarah came from Watford. James was already, or was about to be, living and working in Somerset, for his and Sarah's children had their births recorded in the baptismal register of the parish of West Monkton, just north of Taunton. The eldest, James William, was registered on 14th September 1835, followed by John Corbett on 15th June 1837. A third son, George, was born on 27th April 1839, and was entered in the register on 24th May. The only daughter, Caroline, appears in the baptismal register a year later, on 29th June 1840.[4]

James was gardener at Walford House, one of the four 'principal residences' of West Monkton and owned by Robert Farthing Beauchamp. The house was surrounded, according to the 1868 National Gazetteer of Great Britain and Ireland, by 'an extensive well-wooded park.' The largest garden in the neighbourhood was (and is) Hestercombe and it seems likely that James was also

MARRIAGES solemnized in the Parish of *Paddington* in the County of *Middlesex* in the Year 18*35*

_____ of *this* Parish

and _____ of *this* Parish

were married in this Church by _____ this *twentieth* Day of _____ in the Year One Thousand Eight Hundred and *thirty five* By me *J. S. Gifford, Curate*

This marriage was solemnized between us { *James Duncan* / *Sarah Beige* }

In the presence of { *Wm Peak* / *Jane Peak* }

No. *75*

The above Extract from the Register of Marriages, was made this *28th* Day of *January* 18*35* by me *J. S. Gifford, Curate*

familiar with this garden. Mr Beauchamp, however, died in 1841, and it is possible that his employer's death was the reason for James leaving the area. There is no mention of the family at Walford House in the 1841 census, at which time the only occupants were servants. Today, the house has been converted into flats, and there is little trace of what the grounds might once have been like.

Somerset with its limestone and humid, green valleys must have seemed extraordinarily lush after the granite landscape and east wind of Aberdeenshire. But for his next job, James returned to the north. In 1842, he was appointed gardener at Howick Hall in Northumberland. The estate ledgers of Howick record that he, Sarah and the children travelled north to enable him to start work there in April. He was paid £10 for 'expenses from London with family'. He was now nearly 40.

His new employer was the second Earl Grey, lately prime minister and in retirement in his beloved home near the Northumberland coast. In some ways James must have felt himself closer to his own home – Howick is much nearer to Aberdeen than it is to Somerset, and it shares the same outlook eastwards to the North Sea. However, that is unlikely to have been the reason why James and his family went there. Perhaps the job, which was in effect the post of head gardener, was a promotion; perhaps the move was the result of a personal

encounter or recommendation. Whatever, the reason, James now found himself among the Grey family.

Earl Grey's eldest son, Viscount Howick, wrote in his diary that summer: 'A most boiling day notwithstanding which I worked a good deal in the garden . . . . This has been the hottest day I ever remember in England.'

5

THE GREYS AND THE HOOKERS

Two men in particular influenced James Duncan's later life: a politician and a botanist, the third Earl Grey and Sir William Hooker.

The first Earl Grey had been a soldier. Although he enjoyed a distinguished career, particularly in the American War of Independence, his later career was dogged by an incident which curiously in this context may later have influenced the history of Mauritius. It was alleged in 1794 that Sir Charles Grey, as he then was, had exacted excessive prize money from the conquered French islands in the West Indies (Martinique and Guadaloupe). He was exonerated, but was never given another overseas command. And it is not impossible that this episode was still fresh in people's minds when plans were laid fifteen years later for the conquest of some other French islands, those in the Indian Ocean, the conquest of which was made as painfree as possible for the inhabitants.[1]

His son the second earl, also named Charles, was a raffish man in his youth. Entering politics, he joined Charles James Fox's group of Whigs. It was not long before the somewhat arrogant young politician from Northumberland had started an affair with the woman at the social centre of the Whig party, Georgiana Duchess of Devonshire. Her husband, the duke, openly maintained a mistress, but when Georgiana found herself pregnant by Charles Grey, she was hustled away to the Continent, where a daughter was born in the south of France in February 1792. Given the name of Eliza Courtney, the girl was sent to Grey's family home, where she was brought up by his parents as their own child.[2]

Two years later, Grey married Mary Ponsonby, by whom he had fifteen children, filling the family home of Howick Hall in Northumberland. Succeeding to the title in 1807 on the death of his father, the second earl led a flourishing political career, though he complained endlessly about its frustrations. He had become leader of the Whigs following the death of Fox in 1806, but then had to endure many years of opposition, finally becoming prime minister only in 1830, on the accession to the throne of William IV.

In spite of the fact that the ministers in Grey's government were almost to a man peers, many of them members of his own family, in four years he pushed through the liberal measures on which his political reputation rests, particularly the great reform bills and the act abolishing slavery throughout the British Empire (including, of course, Mauritius). But he was an 18th century Whig aristocrat at heart, and when, in 1834, he finally withdrew from politics and retired to live permanently at Howick, he became increasingly blimpish in his attitude to subsequent reforms: his own reforms had been intended to be the end, not the beginning, of changes to a settled order of society.

Charles Grey was succeeded in 1845 by his son Henry, born in 1802 and therefore the exact contemporary of James Duncan. Under his courtesy title Viscount Howick, the future third earl had an early introduction to Britain's imperial role. Along with other members of the family, his father gave him a post in his 1830 government. In Henry's case, the job was that of under secretary for the colonies. He belonged to a group of colonial reformers who held views that were more liberal than his father found easy to countenance, and in 1834 he resigned, from dissatisfaction that slave emancipation, following energetic representations from plantation owners, was to be made a gradual process. He returned to government the following year under Lord Melbourne, as secretary at war, but resigned again in 1839. According to the 11th edition of *Encyclopaedia Britannica*, 'these repeated resignations gave him a reputation for crotchetiness.'

He was, however, back in government in 1846, this time as secretary of state for the colonies in Lord John Russell's government. Between then and his resignation in 1852, he is said to have been the first minister to proclaim that the colonies were to be governed for their own benefit, and not for the mother country. And it was during this period that he appointed his head gardener, James Duncan, to be the director of the Royal Botanic Garden in Mauritius. He thus kept up the family tradition of patronage.

Henry finally left office in 1852. He published the following year a two volume work entitled *The Colonial Policy of Lord John Russell's Administration*, a detailed analysis and justification of his work on behalf of both the mother country and the colonies. He never held office again. Retiring to Howick, he wrote pamphlets and frequent letters to The Times and lived on until 1894. Although married, he had no sons, and his title passed to his nephew.

The *Encyclopaedia Britannica* summed up his career dismissively in these terms: 'He was generally deemed impracticable and disagreeable.' It is true that he was regarded as a difficult man by his colleagues – and even by his father – but this was not infrequently because his views were far more liberal than was acceptable at the time. His letters, certainly, give a much more congenial impression.

The other great influence on James Duncan's career was Sir William Hooker. Born in 1785, the young William Hooker was an enthusiastic naturalist and from childhood he showed a talent for being in touch with the right people at the right time. He was appointed Professor of Botany in Glasgow in 1820, and remained there for 21 years, becoming perhaps the most eminent botanist in the country, who consciously built up a network of former students spread out through the botanic gardens of the Empire. He was knighted in 1836. His great ambition was to take over Kew, the royal garden which had fallen behind in prestige and expertise since the days of Joseph Banks. In 1841 he realised his ambition, and became first director of the Royal Botanic Garden at Kew, now freed from its role as a private royal domain.

Hooker had an extraordinary number of correspondents: the archives at Kew are said to hold 29,000 letters from 4,420 individuals.[3] Plants and seeds were sent from the colonial gardens to Kew, using newly developed methods of packing to ensure their arrival alive after long sea voyages: the process was not one way and vast quantities of plants and seeds were despatched outwards to the many corresponding institutions. All this was made possible by the invention of the Wardian case by Dr Nathaniel Ward. Made of wood and glass, the cases enclosed a microclimate, the original intention being to allow people living in the smoggy cities of the time to maintain indoors a miniature garden. The cases turned out to be ideal for carrying living plants long distances by sea, though problems arose when the bulky and heavy cases had to be transported from docks to botanic garden, as James Duncan was to discover.[4]

At the same time, Hooker worked with sponsors to send expeditions abroad in search of new plants. In 1843, for example, he sent William Purdie to Central America, jointly financed by Kew and the Duke of Northumberland, Earl Grey's near neighbour.

In 1847, a Museum of Economic Botany was opened at Kew, which attracted specimens from all over the world. And in 1848 the famous Palm House was completed, a great structure in glass which allowed the growth to full size of tropical plants. There was an element of competitiveness in all this. The Kew Palm House was preceded in 1834 by the Tropical Palm House in the Royal Botanic Garden Edinburgh, and in 1840 by Joseph Paxton's 'Great Stove' at Chatsworth.[5] This competitiveness extended to individual plants. In 1849 Kew succeeded in propagating seeds of *Victoria amazonica*, the giant Amazon water-lily, and sent seedlings to Chatsworth. Here, Paxton managed to bring the plant to flower. One of the first blooms was presented personally to Queen Victoria.[6]

Another enthusiastic race was to produce the first flowering in Britain of *Amherstia nobilis*, a leguminous tree that had been discovered in Burma in 1826, a race won by Mrs Lawrence at Ealing Park, where the brilliant red and yellow flowers appeared to everyone's admiration in 1849, to be illustrated in the *Botanical Magazine*. This was among the plants that the newly appointed director of the Botanic Garden of Mauritius, passing through London that year, wanted to introduce into his island, where the climate enabled tropical plants to grow without the protection of glass.

But all this lay in the future. We must return to James Duncan on his way north to his new job in Northumberland.

6

HOWICK HALL

Howick Hall is hidden in folds of countryside that extend from the Northumbrian hills down to the North Sea coast. The house is less than a mile from the sea, and the main East Coast railway passes nearby, yet it feels remarkably secluded. The house today looks southwards across terraces and over lawns to a small lake, formed out of a stream passing along the valley bottom. On the far side, the ground rises gently to a ha-ha, with views of farmland beyond. Surrounding the house are magnificent trees, mature beeches, oaks and yews. To one side is the early Victorian estate church, built in pale ochre stone in the Romanesque style, with decorative round arched windows running the length of the building. Beyond the church, with its surrounding graves of the Grey family and estate workers, is a woodland garden, from which a lane crosses by bridge the local road from Longhoughton to Craster, before narrowing into a path which winds in broad sweeps down a wooded valley towards the sea – the 'Long Walk'. If you walk down it in summer time, the marshy ground on either side of the stream is filled with wildflowers and is shaded by the old beech trees which rise with immensely tall silvery trunks before spreading their branches high above the valley floor. And then at the end of the valley, the sky lightens, and all at once you are on the rocky shore, with a sandy beach stretching away on either side. Turn left, and you follow the path known as the 'Sea Walk' along the rocky coast; and then turning left again you can walk through the small village of Howick, built by the Grey family in the 19th century to replace estate houses that used to surround the Hall itself. The solid buildings are of sandstone with slate roofs, late Georgian in style with a touch of Gothick. They include the former school, with master's house attached, and a terrace of estate workers' houses with a central dovecote.

The Palladian bulk of Howick Hall itself is surprisingly large. The main block, with a central pediment on the south face, is linked to pavilions topped with bellcotes. The south front was the entrance of the original plain, classical building erected in 1782. When Mary and her husband Charles, the future second Earl Grey, moved into the house in 1801, they set about expanding it, building a new entrance to the north. (Much of the north front seen today was, however, rebuilt in the 20th century following a fire which destroyed much of the interior of the house.)

George Wyatt, who carried out the early 19th century rebuilding, also built the first terrace on the south side of the house. This was the latest fashion, introduced by Humphry Repton, which was intended to distance somewhat the surrounding countryside, as opposed to the 18th century concept of a landscaped park running right up to the walls of a house. At the same time, Lord Grey embarked on a woodland planting scheme, which helped to protect the house from the east winds blowing off the sea; but he also had in mind the need at this time of war to plant trees for future potential use by the navy.

In the 1820s and 30s, the house was filled with children. Unusually for the time, Charles and Mary decided not to send any of the fifteen children to school. Instead, they were educated by tutors at Howick, until the time came for (some of) them to go to university. They roamed freely over the surrounding countryside and saw a great deal of their father, who all his life took himself only with reluctance from his home to Westminster.[1]

The house must have seemed much quieter by 1842, the year that James Duncan arrived. The children had all left home, the heir, Viscount Howick, being an active politician himself. Earl Grey was 78 and had only another three years to live.

James's predecessor as head gardener at Howick was one Thomas Stone, who had lasted for less than a year, and before him the post had been occupied by a William Balfour, who had held the job for many years. Thomas Stone had been paid £70 a year, six monthly in arrears. James was employed at the slightly higher salary of £80. Calculating present day equivalents to 19th century sums is an imprecise science, but in terms of average price levels, £80 in 1842 was the equivalent of £5,092 in 2001.[2]

Almost certainly, the Duncan family lived in what is still known as the head gardener's house. (In earlier documents it is referred to as the gardener's house, but that was the title of the job in the 19th century.) It is a handsome two storied late Georgian house of dressed stone. Originally there were only two rooms up and two rooms down, but there is an extension to the back, built at some point in the 19th century. On the right hand wall there is a heavy buttress, indicating subsidence in the past – the house may have been built over a former reservoir.[3]

Behind the house was another for bachelor labourers, and to the left is the former apple house, a substantial building where fruit could be stored during the winter months. Conveniently to hand, under the gardener's eye, were the potting sheds, glasshouses and the walled garden, which at one time extended to four acres. Beyond the walls of the garden can still be seen the somewhat ragged tops of ancient oaks and beeches which survive from James's time.

When the Duncan family arrived at Howick in April 1842, the children were still young, aged 6, 4, nearly 3, and just under 2, so this was perhaps their formative childhood home. The house is only a few hundred metres from the sea, reached by scrambling down a path from the cliff edge. The local rock is mudstone, containing fragments of fossils which were laid down 300 million years ago at a time when Britain was located close to the equator. These flat sheets of rock are ideal for lying or playing on, and the children must surely have explored the area and collected the yellow bird's-foot trefoil and pink thrift that grow there, perhaps learning to draw them. Later, two of the boys, James William and George, put together collections of drawings of Mauritian plants; examples of James William's work are still to be seen at Kew.

Apart from his salary, payments were made to James for the labourers. The number of these is unknown, but they were initially divided into two groups, with a smaller sum for the Garden and a larger one for the Pleasure Grounds. Later the two were combined. These payments were made fortnightly, varying somewhat each time, implying that workers were taken on as required for individual projects. The first payment made through James, on 15th April 1842, was £4.12.0 for the Garden and £17.18.2 for the Pleasure Grounds.[4]

The estate was, of course, a major business. In 1849, the total estate income from rents was £22,679.5.4 – or over £1.6 million at today's price levels. From this, Viscount Howick (as he was still called in the estate accounts) received an annual allowance of £2,000 (£143,000 in today's money). In 1848, not long

before James left Howick, there were also payments made through him to 'old persons', presumably pensioners.

Apart from supervising and paying the garden staff, James received reimbursement for other things, which throws some light on activities in the garden at that time. Soon after he arrived at Howick, he paid J. Wilmot £5.17.0 for dahlias – quite a considerable sum, exceeding the total payment for other 'plants and seeds'. Dahlias were fashionable – in 1837, Joseph Paxton had published a monograph on the flower. In January or February each year there were payments made for beer money for the men filling the ice house. And James seems to have taken over some of the responsibility for the restoration of Howick church which was undertaken by Viscount Howick after he succeeded to the earldom. The existing 18th century classical building was extended, the windows given a Romanesque-style trim, and a bellcote added.[5]

There were other activities unconnected with gardening that James seems to have become engaged in on behalf of the family. Viscount Howick's cousin, Sir George Grey, had inherited in 1845 the nearby estate of Falloden and following his appointment as home secretary by Lord John Russell, he stood for one of the Northumberland parliamentary seats in the August 1847 general election. James Duncan seems to have joined in the election campaign on behalf of Sir George, who won the seat against a protectionist.[6]

According to the biography written by the second earl's younger son, Lieut-General Charles Grey, the former prime minister had maintained control of the garden into old age. 'All planting and thinning till the very last years of his life were conducted under his own superintendence.'[7] His son Henry inherited his interest in gardening, particularly in the early years between his resignation from Melbourne's government in 1839 and his return to office in 1846. In September 1842 he visited Chatsworth in Derbyshire. These were the already famous gardens developed by Joseph Paxton for the Duke of Devonshire. It is conceivable that Grey took the newly appointed head gardener of Howick with him on this tour. In any event, he recorded in his diary:

We have been very much interested by all there was to see the great conservatory (which is really splendid) the kitchen garden etc. . . . We went over the Kitchen with Paxton who explained to us all the arrangements & contrivances he has adopted which are very ingenious, he is obviously a very remarkable man.[8]

In January 1844 he was at Howick, where he 'marked some trees with Duncan.' The following November, he was again 'out marking trees with Duncan today in Little Mill plantation.' Little Mill is still a plantation, currently growing trees planted in the 1950s. It is near today's railway level crossing: three months earlier, the famous engineer Isambard Kingdom Brunel had visited Howick to discuss the development of new railway lines north of Newcastle.

The ledgers record extensive development of the estate during this period. There were improvements to the sea wall, to the extent that Viscount Howick could describe the Sea Walk as 'new' when he mentioned a walk along it in August 1845. The pinetum was developed, with new drainage and bridges. (The cost of a bridge at that time, examples of which can be seen today in the Long Walk, was £1.2.6.[9]) Pinetums were a fashionable addition to large early Victorian gardens. New species of conifer were being introduced into Britain at that time from sources overseas, especially North America, and collectors could put together a wide range of trees which made a striking contrast to the neighbouring largely deciduous woods.[10]

By the 1840s, the avenues of oaks and beeches planted by the former prime minister, survivors from among which are still visible today, would have been of a reasonable size. Part of James's responsibilities would have been maintaining these plantings in good order. During his visits to Howick, Henry drove his father on tours through the garden and down the Long Walk. One wonders

whether James remembered these impressive rows of trees when planning his own palm avenues in the very different surroundings of Mauritius.

In July 1845, Viscount Howick was in London. Hearing that his father was very ill, he took the mail train to Newcastle, and then travelled on to Alnwick, arriving at 1.15 in the morning. A carriage met him to take him to Howick, where several of his brothers were already installed. His father died on July 17th. The funeral was held in the estate church.

> The church was quite full but almost exclusively of people belonging to the place. . . . After luncheon I walked with Frederick & Wood to the sea & sat a long time with the latter on the rocks talking of all sorts of things.[11]

Henry was now the third Earl Grey and soon afterwards he joined Lord John Russell's government as secretary of state for the colonies. The issues with which he was faced in that post were not the equal of the overwhelming tragedy of the time, the potato failure and subsequent famine in Ireland, but increasingly the British government was having to take on responsibility for an expanding collection of colonies, including those where slavery had only recently been abolished. The new earl was keen to justify his actions and to be understood, and no sooner had he (along with the rest of the government) left office in 1852, than he set about writing a book of almost 900 pages which outlined in the form of letters addressed to the former prime minister not only the principles that underlay his colonial policy, but detailed analyses of each colony.[12]

The basic principle was clear. Grey was a firm believer in free trade, throughout the Empire, not just within Britain, and he argued forcefully against the opinion that had previously held sway, that the economic relationship between a mother country and her colonies should be based on monopolies and tariffs against third parties. One of his first measures was an Act of 1846 which provided for the immediate reduction and eventual abolition of the differential duty on foreign sugar. This had a major effect on sugar colonies like Mauritius, already in a state of some turmoil resulting from the fact that following abolition of slavery in 1833, the former slaves were (perhaps not surprisingly) unenthusiastic about carrying out the same work as before, though now for wages. However, Grey believed himself fully justified in his policies by the very substantial *increase* of sugar imports from Mauritius to Britain between 1846 and 1851.

Grey was also keen to emphasise that self-interested patronage no longer played a part in the work of a secretary of state. He listed the 35 colonies to which he had appointed governors or lieutenant-governors during his term of office, including two to Mauritius, drawing attention to the number of individuals who were personally unknown to him at the time of their appointment.[13] Perhaps he was all too aware of the criticism his father had incurred on account of the number of members of his own family that he had appointed to his government in 1830.

On 29th January, 1849 Grey had an audience with the Queen in order to propose to her George Anderson as the new governor of Mauritius. In the post, on its way from the Indian Ocean, was a letter from the outgoing governor, reporting the death of Mr Newman, director of the Botanic Garden, and requesting that a successor be sent from Britain. Grey in his book was to claim that apart from the governors themselves, very few offices should be filled with nominations by the secretary of state, even though in theory he controlled all offices with a salary worth over £200 a year. In spite of this, on 1st May, he appointed his Howick head gardener, James Duncan, to the Mauritian post.

James was not entirely enthusiastic about taking the job, it would seem with good reason. Lord Grey wrote to the governor:

> I have informed Mr Duncan that in accepting this appointment he must consider the salary as liable to reduction if it should be found necessary to include it in any general scheme for the reduction of salaries in the colony,

but I have at the same time stated to him that I did not suppose any such general reduction could be to a greater extent than 10 per cent on existing salaries.

I find that with the prospect of even this reduction Mr Duncan had much hesitation in accepting the appointment, & that there would be little prospect of obtaining the services of a competent person in so expensive a colony at a lower rate hence if a reduction of the emoluments of this situation should appear to be requisite it ought not to exceed that which I have mentioned.[14]

James's last appearance in the Howick ledgers was on 26th June 1849, when he received his final wage of £26.13.4 for four months work. His successor was called Fred. Moore.

In September that year, Queen Victoria visited Howick, planted a canary oak, and was taken in a pony carriage down Long Walk, along Sea Walk, and through the village. But by then James had gone.

7

To Mauritius

James Duncan (and his family) must have travelled straight south from Howick, without paying a visit to Aberdeen, for by 4th July he was in London. It would seem from a letter written by Sir William Hooker many years later that Lord Grey initially sent James to be vetted by the eminent botanist John Lindley, in order to ascertain whether he (James Duncan) would meet the governor of Mauritius's request for a 'common but good practical gardener'.[1] Lindley having approved him, Grey confirmed the appointment, and only then asked James to visit Sir William Hooker at Kew. He wrote to him as follows:

> My dear Sir —
>   The bearer of this note (Mr Duncan) is the person who is just going to Mauritius to take charge of the Botanical garden in that colony, he has been a good many years head gardener at Howick & I therefore know that he thoroughly understands his business.— I have desired him to call upon you in order that if there shd be any plants you may wish that he shd send for Kew or any instructions that you may think it right to give him you may have the opportunity of doing so.
>   I am faithfully yrs
>   Grey[2]

It would appear from this letter that Lord Grey did not at the time know Hooker personally and, as we have seen, it was he who personally chose James Duncan for the Mauritian post. This cannot have been altogether welcome to Hooker, who was already to a large extent at the controlling centre of a web of colonial gardens spread around the globe. Wherever possible, he placed Kew trained botanists in the directorial posts. James was neither Kew trained, nor a botanist.

A few days later Grey wrote again.

My dear Sir William

I am much obliged to you for having been so good as to see Duncan & to give him instructns respecting his duties; I will certainly give him a letter of introductn to the Governor to whom I think it is very desirable that you shd write also as you propose. —

I suppose the [illeg.] grass may be of much value in Mauritius, but as that colony seldom suffers from drought perhaps it wd be still more important to send it to Western Australia where from the accounts we receive they seem to be much in want of a grass which will resist their very hot & dry summers. – A ship is about to sail for this colony almost immediately, & as the opportunities of communicating with it are not frequent I shd be glad to send some of the plants or seeds now. —

I am faithfully yrs

Grey

In fact, the ship had already left, so the plants for Australia had to wait. But meanwhile, Hooker was having doubts about the appointment. Grey wrote once more:

Private   July 25/49

My dear Sir,—

I understand that you have expressed some doubt as to the fitness of Duncan for the place of manager of the Botanical Garden in Mauritius to which I have just appointed him & I am therefore anxious to explain to you what are the reasons which have influenced me in my selectn. — I found upon enquiry that for the salary of 250£ in so expensive a colony it wd be quite impossible to expect any gentleman of scientific education to accept & hold the appointment, & also that the services of such a gentleman are not in fact required. — What is wanted as I learn from persons well acquainted with the Island is a good practical cultivator there being in the Committee by which the Garden is superintended two or three gentlemen of much scientific knowledge who can supply whatever is wanted in this respect. — As a practical cultivator I have no doubt of Duncan's skill, it is impossible to be more successful in this way than he has been at Howick.

I am faithfully yrs

Grey

This letter is interesting on several counts. Firstly, from early in his stay in Mauritius, James was to complain about the high cost of living, and about how his salary was insufficient for the job he was being asked to do. Secondly, the 'gentlemen of much scientific knowledge' seem to have evaporated by the time James arrived. The person who might best have filled that role was Dr Bojer, who was certainly qualified but who seems to have been rather unhelpful, as we will see. Finally, the tension between Hooker's wish to see trained botanists placed in all the key gardens overseas and the wish of the local administrators to employ efficient (and less expensive) gardeners was played out again at the very end of Hooker's life, when James retired. James himself never claimed to be a botanist, even though his experiences in Mauritius began to turn him into one.

The final letter from Grey to Hooker in this exchange is evidence of Hooker's lifelong skill in building a network of useful contacts in debt to him. With exotic plants arriving monthly at Kew from overseas collectors, he was in an excellent position to distribute them in a way that was advantageous to him – and to Kew.

Howick Dec 21

Lord and Lady Grey present their compts to Sir William Hooker & beg that he will accept their very best thanks for the collection of plants he has been so very good as to send them & which is infinitely larger than they had expected — Lady Grey is quite delighted with them.[3]

Meanwhile, almost at once James came up against the sort of financial problem that was to dog him later. He must have been staying in London at Earl Grey's house in Belgrave Square, or at least using it as a base, for on 27th July, just two days after Grey wrote to Hooker concerning the latter's doubts about the appointment, James himself wrote a letter to Hooker from number 30 Belgrave Square. He expressed his best thanks for the interest Hooker had taken on his behalf, but told him that he had learned that there was no way in which his passage money was going to be paid in Britain, Grey saying that 'there is no funds in this country available for the purpose'. Could Hooker help by sending letters to officials in Mauritius on his behalf? James added: 'After I reach the Island and get a little settled I hope to have the pleasure of occasionally writing to you.' [4]

A few days later, James and his family set sail on board the *Blumette*, accompanied by two glazed (Wardian) cases, containing 46 plant specimens and seeds of assorted fruits and vegetables, supplied by the Horticultural Society in Chiswick for the use of the Botanic Garden in Mauritius. Among the plants were ten varieties of rose and a dozen vines, both white and black, including chasselas, muscat, and frontignan. The selection of seeds optimistically included gooseberries and strawberries.

For some reason, the boat was delayed during the passage. James told Sir William Hooker in a letter sent a year later, that the journey took an unusual five months, and the family did not arrive in Mauritius until 28th December.[5] It was very likely an uncomfortable journey. This was near the end of the sailing ship

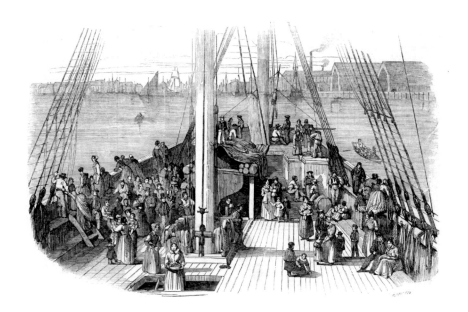

era, and when ten years later James corresponded with Kew about a proposed assistant, he recommended with feeling that the new man should travel out by P & O steamer and not on a sailing ship. 'On board these steamers there is plenty of good provisions, medical attendance, etc etc, & these things at sea are of very great importance to health and comfort.' They were easily overtaken on their voyage by the mail boat, *Briton's Queen*: this carried a letter from Lord Grey to Sir George Anderson dated 25th August, which arrived in Mauritius on 18th November.[6] The usual route at that time was round the Cape of Good Hope, following the trade route between Europe and India that had been the setting for the colonial wars of the 18th and early 19th centuries. By now, the map was coloured red in the various imperial island possessions which the ship passed. It was only in 1856 that the first steamers started carrying passengers from Mauritius to Europe via Aden (the 'overland' route).

Thirteen years earlier, in 1836, Charles Darwin had visited Mauritius towards the end of his celebrated voyage on the *Beagle*. He published a record of his arrival there, and this must represent something very similar to what the Duncan family saw when they finally reached their destination.

April 29th. – In the morning we passed round the northern end of Mauritius, or the Isle of France. From this point of view the aspect of the island equalled the expectations raised by the many well-known descriptions of its beautiful scenery. The sloping plain of the

Pamplemousses, interspersed with houses, and coloured by the large fields of sugar-cane of a bright green, composed the foreground. The brilliancy of the green was the more remarkable because it is a colour which generally is conspicuous only from a very short distance. Towards the centre of the island groups of wooded mountains rose out of this highly cultivated plain; their summits, as so commonly happens with ancient volcanic rocks, being jagged into the sharpest points. Masses of white clouds were collected around these pinnacles, as if for the sake of pleasing the stranger's eye. The whole island, with its sloping border and central mountains, was adorned with an air of perfect elegance: the scenery, if I may use such an expression, appeared to the sight harmonious.

I spent the greater part of the next day in walking about the town and visiting different people. The town is of considerable size, and is said to contain 20,000 inhabitants; the streets are very clean and regular. Although the island has been so many years under the English government, the general character of the place is quite French: Englishmen speak to their servants in French, and the shops are all French; indeed I should think that Calais or Boulogne was much more Anglified. There is a very pretty little theatre in which operas are excellently performed. We were also surprised at seeing large booksellers' shops, with well-stored shelves; — music and reading bespeak our approach to the old world of civilisation; for in truth both Australia and America are new worlds.

The various races of men walking in the streets afford the most interesting spectacle in Port Louis. Convicts from India are banished here for life; at present there are about 800, and they are employed in various public works. Before seeing these people, I had no idea that the inhabitants of India were such noble-looking figures. Their skin is extremely dark, and many of the older men had large mustaches and beards of a snow-white colour; this, together with the fire of their expression gave them quite an imposing aspect. The greater number had been banished for murder and the worst crimes; others for causes which can scarcely be considered as moral faults, such as for not obeying, from superstitious motives, the English laws. These men are generally quiet and well-conducted; from their outward conduct, their cleanliness and faithful observance of their strange religious rites, it was impossible to look at them with the same eyes as on our wretched convicts in New South Wales. . . .

May 5th – Captain Lloyd took us to the Rivière Noire, which is several miles to the southward, that I might examine some rocks of elevated coral.

We passed through pleasant gardens, and fine fields of sugar-cane growing amidst huge blocks of lava. The roads were bordered by hedges of Mimosa, and near many of the houses there were avenues of the mango. Some of the views where the peaked hills and the cultivated farms were seen together were exceedingly picturesque; and we were constantly tempted to exclaim "How pleasant it would be to pass one's life in such quiet abodes!" Captain Lloyd possessed an elephant, and he sent it half-way with us, that we might enjoy a ride in true Indian fashion. The circumstance which surprised me most was its quite noiseless step. This elephant is the only one present on the island; but it is said others will be sent for.[7]

The distant view of the island is the same today, and the little theatre survives – built in 1822, it is the oldest surviving lyric theatre in the southern hemisphere. Visiting French companies and local amateur groups performed there and for the opening season a Creole group performed both a play and *Maison à vendre*, one of Nicolas-Marie Dalayrac's most popular *opéras comiques*.[8]

8

SAFE ARRIVAL

The village of Pamplemousses is situated 11 kilometres north of Port Louis, on a fertile plain with good views of the eccentrically shaped hills surrounding the capital. Before the end of James's stay on the island, a railway was built, but in the early days journeys to Port Louis – and to its docks – had to be made by road.

Le Port-Louis, vu du large.

Where did James and his family live when they arrived in Mauritius? As we have seen, the house of Mon Plaisir was not available, being no longer part of the Garden. However, the government had bought from John Newman the house and land which he owned at the south-western end of the Botanic Garden as it exists today, near the junction of the Flacq and Mapou roads. This land became known as Le Petit Jardin, and the house on it was described as being suitable for immediate occupation by the director of the Garden: 'It is well situated and of good construction.'[1]

The house may have been easy to move into when the family first arrived, but in 1853 James reported to the colonial secretary in Port Louis, that the roof was in a bad state and needed repair. In a tropical climate, subject to cyclones, wooden buildings could deteriorate fast and in 1865, after James had left Mauritius, the house was claimed to be in such poor condition that there was a question of rebuilding it. His successors, Charles Meller and John Horne, did continue to live there, but in 1877 Horne wrote that his health had suffered 'for having lived permanently at Pamplemousses where for some years fever has been endemic'. All the same, in the 1890s the director William Scott was still living in the house, where he entertained General Gordon, 'the hero of Khartoum'.

The island as a whole had seen some important changes since Darwin's visit in 1836. The Revd Francis Flemyng, military chaplain in 1854, greatly regretted the alterations that had been made to the natural environment, and, in particular, the manner in which plant introductions had been made. 'The flora of the island is varied, and at certain seasons pretty,' he wrote. 'The gardens (save the public ones at Pamplemousses) are, however, very tasteless and uninteresting.'[2]

In particular, Flemyng was unhappy with the obsession with sugar which had gripped the island. His description of the countryside seems rather hard to reconcile with Darwin's positive view, written only twenty years before; but it is worth noting that in those twenty years, the production of sugar had increased threefold, the clearing of land for sugar canes leading to an inevitable alteration in the landscape.[3]

James took his time before reporting to higher authorities what he found in the Botanic Garden itself on his arrival, and in fact it was almost a year before he made his first formal reports to London. However, he seems to have wasted no time in writing home to Aberdeen. It is a pity that this letter has not survived, but we do have his father's reply, which is dated May 1850, so James must have written no later than March. William's letter provides both valuable family news and a first hand description of conditions in Aberdeen, which was enduring economic depression along with the rest of the country. The textile boom had ended, largely as a result of increased competition from elsewhere, aided by the arrival of new rail connections. However, these were in due course to benefit the cattle trade, by offering quicker routes to southern markets. Aberdeen's first formal cattle auction mart was in King Street, not far from William Duncan's house at Berryden.

Mill-bank Cottage
Aberdeen 19 May 1850

My dear Son

We were very much gratified on receiving three or four days ago your long looked for letter for I was getting very anxious upon your account, only the delay is easily accounted for by your long long passage and the letter itself being about 4 months in reaching this. –

I am very glad that you have reached your destination all well 'thank God for that', it is indeed something to be grateful for, and that you find things pretty comfortable about you, and a little patience with the French tongue will get over that difficulty, in fact even at present were you to be set down in the middle of Paris I fancy you could make yourself pretty comfortable if asking could enable you to be so, but I daresay Mrs. Duncan will find it rather troublesome to remember if the tablecloth and your snuffbox and these sort of things are male or female, however its of no use wasting time or feather paper in guessing what you are about while all the time you are wondering what we are doing.— At last we have got the Railway into Aberdeen or Ferry hill rather, it is a great public convenience but is not paying well. The North Line is still talked about but Railway property is so bad in the mean time that I dont think it can go on. The Docks are now finished and between the Steam Boats and the Railway we send off from 500 to 600 head of cattle every week. There is a thing often spoken about in Aberdeen been started lately with great success, I mean the deep sea fishing as it is called. That is going out in Smacks to the Dogger bank some 20 miles off the Girdleness and returning in a couple of days with a cargo of fine white fish.

Free trade is getting rather at a discount in this country now and the Protectionists are forming themselves into a league headed by the Duke of Richmond a la Cobden, however, they were defeated in Parliament the other evening by a Majority of 114 so that from the present Parliament they have nothing to look for, only if things go on as they are now doing the next election may give a different result.— Trade is still very flat here and Emigration going on vigorously, it is understood that six steam boats of 2,000 tons each are to be built here and there over the Kingdom by this time next year to carry the West Indian Mails at an increased rate of speed, which will help to give some employment. William Riddel is still with Mr. Gibb but while there was 30 in that office some three years ago there are but three now, and Civil Engineering is much in this state all over the kingdom. I had a letter from Mr. Head from the Rectory at Howick about six weeks ago asking very kindly after you, and sent an answer at the time saying, of course, we had only got a newspaper and wrote again the day after receiving your letter giving him the *heads* of it.—

We have sent to the Mauritius a newspaper at different times since you left England perhaps half a dozen in all, and there is one sent along with this letter, write if you get them regularly and I will send one frequently, not to let the children forget about their Fatherland altogether for I suppose England and Scotland are much the same to you now.—

I regret to tell you of the sudden death of my Brother John on the 1st. February at Beildside about 5 miles from Aberdeen up the Deeside Road, he had taken his dinner as usual apparently in good health, and after sitting down to his work fell over in a few minutes afterwards quite dead, he was interred in the Spital burying-ground at my expense as he left nothing behind him.—

On account of the long time that had elapsed before hearing from you I got rather impatient and as a *dernier resort* wrote to Harrow weald and received in reply that they had heard nothing of you and that Mrs. Duncan's Brother was dead which I was very sory to hear and by the bye how comes it that in your letter there is neither mention of kith nor kin? Mind in your next I shall like to learn how Mrs. Duncan feels after being transplanted and if she has began to take root yet, seriously I should like you to touch a little more upon family matters in the time to come.—

As regards the crop last year the potatoes were a decided improvement upon the two or three preceeding years, the berries were rather a scanty crop but I was pretty well with them and upon the whole it was a good year for me.—

This spring has been terribly cold and backward on the 6th. of May we had ice thick enough to carry a person it nipped the potatoes that were above ground and I am afraid injured a good deal of the fruit.— We had a letter some three months ago from Arthur Harrow asking particularly about you, and mentioning that your successor was a very quiet man but that Howick was not like the same place as formerly, and stating his intention of leaving it soon.— James Riddel and his family are all quite well and send their well wishes only you forgot them among other things in your letter.— I am sorry to tell you that James Shepherd is very much reduced both in health and circumstances, he has lost the peice of ground that he had and I had to pay fifteen pounds for him.—

Otherwise things have thriven pretty well with me since you left this only Vegetables and Garden produce are selling very low in the mean time but provisions are low also the 4 lb loaf selling at 5d. and in some places at 4d.—

Grand mother's compliments to Mrs Duncan and would prize a few lines from her very highly and would also like a close written note from James describing what he is doing and his manner of life — Grandmère has been very poorly this winter but is now a good deal stronger again — I am sorely troubled with a pain in my side at times and a most distressing cough which is like to get the better of me altogether sometimes — I can assure you I feel the distance between us very much, besides when we could have seen each other for a little expence and time, only it cant be helped and is therefore needless to repine, you will see that I have got William Riddel to write this for me as it would take me a long time to write a letter of this kind and my cough is rather troublesome to night.—

Helen you will see speaks for herself, and William Riddel desires to be kindly remembered to yourself and Mrs. Duncan, hoping she has not quite forgot old Scotland also to James John George and little Caroline J'espere elle est tres bein there — what think you of that from *Vieux Grandpere?* —

And now Dear James I must have done, in your next write close and give me a long account about your Island, how you like it and if the change is likely to be advantageous to you, I expect quite a family packet with some contribution from every member, and mind the whole of you to write close

— I expect another letter from you in about a month or six weeks and will answer it in due course — And now Dear James with kind wishes from all here I say good bye and may God bless you and yours is the parting wish of

Your affecanate Father
William Duncan

Since writing the above I have another letter from Mr. Head glad to hear of you and promising to send me word when *he* hears from you.[4]

Since no letters written by James to his family back in Britain have yet been found, it is impossible to know whether he responded to his father's plea for more news, or not.

9

FIRST REPORTS

The governor of Mauritius at the time of James's arrival was the recently appointed Sir George Anderson, who had been presented by Earl Grey to Queen Victoria at an audience the previous January. Grey wrote to the governor from the Colonial Office on 24th April 1850.

My dear Sir George -

I recd. yesterday your private letters of Jan. 16 and 17 & Feb 21 wh. all reached me together – This mail has brought me so many letters from various quarters that I have not time to do more than to thank you for yours & to express my satisfaction at receiving such good accounts of the state of affairs in the Colony – I am sorry to say that on the subject of the currency & the value of the notes I am still unable to furnish you with instructions, the difference of opinion between myself & the Bd. of Treasury being an obstacle to arriving at any definite conclusion wh. has not yet been overcome – The various other matters to wh. you advert shall be attended to as speedily as possible, but during the period of the Session of Parlt. & with the Ceylon Committee & the bill for granting constitutions to the Australian Colonies both in progress I am compelled to postpone all matters wh. are not very urgent & wh. require much consideration -

I am exceedingly glad to hear that you think Duncan is likely to prove a useful man in charge of the Botanical Garden – I can answer for his being a very successful practical gardener. Pray tell him when you may happen to see him that I shall be glad if he will occasionally write to me & let me know how he is getting on -

Grey[1]

So James seems to have made a favourable first impression. The message was passed by the governor, and James did in due course write to his former employer, as we will see shortly. But meanwhile there was work to be done, as this letter sent down to Port Louis shows.

Royal Botanic Gardens
October 15th. 1850

To the Honourable

    The Colonial Secretary

Sir

    I respectfully beg to represent to you that the Tools belonging to the Gardens are becoming much worn. Some of them are allmost useless; I therefore beg that those articles that are worthy of it may be repaired and new ones supplied to replace the others, I herewith enclose a list of such articles as I think would be worth repairing and also a list of the new ones required.

    I have the honour to be

    Sir

Your most Obedient
Humble Servant
James Duncan

P.S. There is sufficient funds allready voted for this purpose.[2]

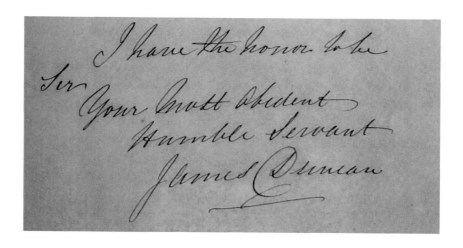

The attached list is detailed and lengthy. Not many of the tools were deemed by James worthy to be repaired, merely 4 plant cases, 2 large stone hammers to be new steeled and 6 'wattering pots' needing new bottoms. The new items required included: 100 garden pots one foot deep and wide for sowing seeds in, 20 hoes, 6 Dutch hoes, 12 bill hooks, 12 sickles, 2 scythes, 6 large padlocks, 12 saw files, 2 hand saws, 3 pruning knives and a cask of nails.

In the government offices in Port Louis, the Assistant Colonial Secretary passed the request on to the Auditor General, who replied that the application might be complied with 'only after an estimate of the cost has been sent in for approval.' The application was passed to the Acting Surveyor General for this purpose, and he produced a figure of £43.11.10d. The Auditor General did not like the look of that, and clearly disagreed with James's P.S., for he minuted: 'The Estimate now under reference exceeds that for the Garden for the Current Year by £28.14.0. The Director must therefore limit his Expenditure to £15. A large amount having been estimated for next year, he will then be able to complete his purchases.'

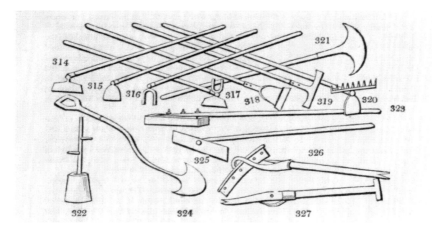

James had in this way an early introduction to colonial civil service systems and to the famously tight control over expenditure maintained by the colonial government in Mauritius.

A fortnight after this application for new tools was sent to Port Louis, James wrote a very full report to his former employer in London, describing the state of the Garden when he arrived.

Royal Botanic Gardens
Pamplemousses
Mauritius
Nov. 1st . 1850

My Lord

By order of His Excellency Sir G. W. Anderson I will endeavour to give your Lordship a description of this Garden, together with its wants its use & its abuses.

First

The Garden contains about 50 Acres of Land and Water, several acres is at present useless in consequence of it being often overflowed by a stream of water that pases through it. This could be cured by widening & deepening its channel, a great part of it is as compleet a jungle as could be found in any native forest. I have lately opened some walks through this part of it, a small portion had been planted with Nutmeg and Clove-Trees, a great number of native Trees has been allowed to grow up amongest them and spoil them very much. The remaining part is covered with Palms, Bambous, Mangoes, Cinnamon, as well as many native trees, all apperantly self sown, they consequantly stand in no kind or order or regularity. Their is many clove trees amongest them, but generally the native self sown plants have been allowed to overtop & all but destroy them.

Some years back a public Road that passed along one side of the Garden, hade a Bridge carried away by a flood, a Road was opened through the garden till the Bridge could be reabuilt — the said Bridge has however never been reabuilt, and the Road remains through the Garden dividing it in two which would be a great inconvenience were the Garden to be again put in proper order — Their is no fences arround the Garden, nor even a gate at the entrance — The Walks have never been stoned or gravelled, the soil being of an adhesive nature they cannot be walked on in wet weather. Their is no plant in the Garden either named or numbered, in fact this Garden may be called a forest with some openings through it called walks.

Secondly as to its use

There is no nursery on the Island, consequently this is the only place where the Inhabitants can get plants or seeds from, I have distributed upwards of 1000 plants per month ever since I came here, besides cases that have been sent full of plants to Calcutta, Bombay, The Cape, Port Natal, Hobert Town & Sydney, as vessels sails from this Port to nearly every part of the world with Sugar, this would be an excellent central depot for plants as they could be afterwards sent to any Colony, all Tropical plants would grow well here, in this Garden The Thermometer has never been below 68 degrees since wee came here, and sometimes it has been as high as 90 degrees, I alude to the temperature at night; on the higher grounds it is however often much colder, It would also be very usefull as a Promenade for the Public their being no other place of the kind here, but ware it of no other use, the introduction and distribution of usefull & ornemental plants would alone be of great service to the Colony, The Public are generally very fond of planting & ornementing their places if they could get plants — They are also very anxious that this Garden should be again put in order.— Thirdly as to its abuses

They are intirely owing to the evil disposed fact of the public having free access to the Garden from all parts, and at all times, if I plant a new or choice plant in a few days it is cut to pieces and afterwards carried away, so that is quite dishartning to attempt doing anything at presant, I have a small spot of ground near my house where I am obliged to keep all my choice little plants. —

Fourthly as to its wants

A Bridge should be built and the Public Road turned into its former course, The Garden should be properly fenced round, either by building a wall or by planting a living fence, if the latter was to be adopted the ground would require to be cleared of Trees for some distance all round, the ground trenched before planting. — Gates should also be put at the entrance with a lodge for some person to live in to keep the gates shut, Proper regulations should be made as to when the Public is to be admitted.

Part of the Garden should be cleared of the useless trees at present growing on it, the Ground trenched and afterwards planted with a choice collection of Plants from all countries, properly numbered and a Catalogue made, another portion might be made a flower Garden for the cultivation of flowering plants, which the Inhabitants are very fond of, another portion might be set aside for growing all kind of native plants. Some of the sugar planters are anxious that a part of it should be set appart for Sugar Cane, for trying experiments with the kinds of cane at present here as well as for introducing new kind to be afterwards distributed among them. Two mules and a cart should be alloweed for the use of the garden, at present if I have to send away a case of plants, if I cannot borrow a mule & cart, I must pay 7/6 out of my own pocket to hire one, to take it to Town, and everything in the Garden must at present be carried on mens' heads which is a great waste of time & labour — Garden Pots and frames for probigation should be allowed me, a proper assistant should also be allowed me as attending to all corespondance, probigating plants, looking out & packing up plants, is more than I can well accomplish (a number of people are allways asking me to go and see their places & give them my advice but I have little time & no conveyance at present allowed me.)

My presant assistant is a couloured person, he is a very quiet man and very useful for keeping the Malabars at their work (as they will do nothing without a person being constantly with them) but he is of very little use for anything besides. The number of men at present allowed me is 19 Malabar Indians they are paid £1.4.0 each per month. —

After the Garden was once put in order I think about 30 men would keep it in order well, a much larger number would be required to put it in order, This additional number might be supplied from a Prison about 2 miles from the Garden, called the Powder Mill Prison, their is generally a great number of Malabar Prisoners there, often a 100 & upwards, cutting down trees & trenching ground would be very good employment for them, & their labour would be no additional expence, at present I believe they scarcely know how to employ them, — Should the above suggestions be approved off and carried out, which could be done at a small expence, this Garden instead of its being a disgrace to the Crown & the Colony, would soon be a credit to both & would certainly be of great use to this Colony, as well as to many others, and even to England as plants could be sent here from more distant countrys and afterwards sent home, It would be a great accomodation to me as well as to all persons situated like me, to be allowed to receive Letters post free, as well as to be allowed to Frank Letters, they are very expensive here and all letters I have to pay out of my own pocket; were the above privilege allowed me I could both send & receive many kinds of seeds that would be very usefull to both parties, wheras at present they are generally kept till a favourable appertunity offers of sending them, and the consequence is they are generally spoiled & seldom vegetate —

I shall now endeavour to explain to your Lordship how this Garden got into such a ruinous state. After Mr. Newman the late Superintendant came to the Mauritius, it was thought it would be very desirable to have a Kitchen Garden added to the establishment, so as to train up a number of young men as Gardeners to be afterwards distributed amongst the principal Inhabitants as they might require them, 50 acres of excellent ground was accordingly set appart for the purpose, a short distance from the Botanic

Garden. & Mr. Newman went to reside their, his Salary being considered much too low for this Colony in consequance of the very high price of provisions — as an adition to his salary he was allowed to sell the produce for his own benefit. which doubtless added greatly to his income. This all went on very well as long as Slavery lasted and plenty of men could could [sic] be got — upward of 70 men was at the time employed in the two gardens with a Horse and some Oxen. However when slavery was put a stop to & the former slaves would not work, labourers became very scarce, and exceedingly expensive, — It was then determined not to keep on the two gardens. Mr. Newman <u>then got a free grant of the 50 acres of Kitchen Garden & orchard for himself, to keep it on as a Garden for himself</u> [underlined later in pencil, perhaps by Lord Grey], or dispose of it as he pleased. The number of Garden Men was then considerabelly reduced — Mr Newman however kept on the Kitchen Garden where he continued to reside & people say he employed nearly all the men allowed for the Botanic Garden on his own property — be that is it may, the garden and everything in it soon went to ruin, many and loud complaints ware made about it, at length a Commitee was formed by order of the the Governor to consult with Mr. Newman as to the best means of putting the Garden into order again — The Committee & him however didnot agree in their oponions, and ultamatly quarreled, when instead of doing something for the poor Garden, they employed their time in abusing each other & the consequance was nothing was done for the Garden — The Public say they could get no plants from it, that they were obliged to send to Bourbon & other places for what plants they wanted, & they ware consequantly very much displeased with Mr. Newman & the Garden. —

A short time before Mr. Newman died the Governor insisted upon him coming to reside near the Garden, he accordingly removed to the House where I am now living, he was then however in such ill health that so far as the Botanic Garden was concerned it didnot matter much where he lived — This is a small spot of Barren ground perhaps about four Acres, it has never been cultivated nor can much be done with it, as it is nothing but rock & red clay, about one acre of it is water —

Mr. Newman purchased the ground many years ago & bought an old house and built on it, and planted it with Trees, untill a short time before his Death he let it to a Doctor who lived in it, Government gave £1000 for it which was twice as much as it was worth —

I regret very much I have no good land adjoining my house to grow vegetables in for my own use, this soil is however so bad that it would not be worth cultivating.

I have the honour to be

My Lord

Your Lordships

Most obedient

Humble Servant

James Duncan[3]

The letter came to this abrupt end on a personal note, and Lord Grey must have wondered where to keep it. In the event, he filed it in the office, with a covering note: 'The enclosed private letter from Mr Duncan contains information respecting the Botanical Garden at Mauritius so likely to be useful that I think it right to leave it in the office. 22.2.51'

The document indeed sets out what came to pass during the next dozen years. James built his surrounding fence, his grand entrance gate and a lodge. He collected plants from all over the world, sent plants back to Britain, and made plants available to the local public. He published a complete catalogue of the plants in the Botanic Garden. And he created a pleasing place in which to promenade, to such an extent that the Garden at Pamplemousses became one of the main attractions of Mauritius. Yet at the same time, he was never given all the resources he wanted, and throughout his stay on Mauritius he had problems with what he regarded as the penny pinching civil servants in Port Louis.

Now began the correspondence between James, the local colonial administration, and Sir William Hooker at Kew. It is a pity that none of Hooker's letters to James seem to have survived. It would have been interesting to have learned just how it was that he inspired such loyalty among his widespread correspondents. Certainly, Hooker was the recipient of James's most intimate surviving correspondence. The exchange began just a week after James wrote his report to Lord Grey; he now described for Sir William in turn the state in which he had found the Garden when he arrived.

Sir William

I make no doubt but you will have been expecting to hear from me for some time back but really ever since I came here I have had but little time & moreover I felt so disgusted with the Garden that I didnot know what to think or say about it, I am sure you have no idea of the wretched state it is in — it has no fence round it, nor even a gate at the entrance, & a public road passes through the middle, a great Portion of it is as complete a jungle as could be found in any native forest – The walks have never been stoned, graveld nor edged, & in wet weather they cannot be walked upon, in fact it is just a forest. — The plants have no appearance of having ever been named or numbered & the self sown native trees & climbers have been allowed to overgrow everything — The only thing that can be done with a great part of it now is to cut down the wild plants & trench the ground & afterwards replant it, in fact a great portion of it must be made anew.

By the request of the late Governor Sir G. W. Anderson, I have written to Earl Grey & given his Lordship every particular respecting its presant state, as well as what I think should be done, & should his Lordship think proper to recommend its being again restored to its original state of Beauty & usefullness I have no doubt but that it will be done — as many of the inhabitants are very anxious it should be done. They complain that formerly they could get no plants from the Garden, but since I came here I have distributed upwards of 1000 per month & if we hade a better collection our distribution would be very great [illegible.] I however find a great difficulty in probigating some of the plants as I have no frames nor Garden pots. Frames are quite as necessary for probigating plants here as they are in England, — but I hope you will use your influence with Earl Grey to get the Garden put upon a different footing altogether, the expence of doing it would not be great, at present if I wish to send away a box or a case of plants I must pay 7/6d out of my own pocket for the hire of a cart to take them to Town, Pamplemousses is seven miles from Port Louis.

I have packed a box about 3 feet long for you marked B.G. No. 518 and marked specimens of natural history for Sir W.J. Hooker Kew. I will send it on Board The Lord Haddo, Capt. Smith, She sails for England on Saturday first, I think she generally goes into the St Katherine's Docks, This letter will be posted for you as soon as she reaches London, you hade better therefor send some person as soon as possible after receiving this letter to clear the box and bring it away, The Captain being a friend of mine I do not think he will charge anything for taking it to London, providing you clear it & give him no trouble with it, — The Box contains a Bottle of preserved Nutmegs, a Scape in fruit, & also one in flower of the Sagus Ruffia, a fruit with the seeds of Lecythis Minor, a seed pod of Beaumontia Grandiflora, a Spath with the flower not opened & one in fruit of Euterpe oleracea, & a white Ants nest, all of which I hope will be usefull for your Museum, I have also sent a lot of seeds perhaps you will find something interesting amongst them. As other things are to be got I will send you more, If you could send me a lot of clear bottles with large stoppers I could preserve and send you a number of Fruits in the same way as I have done the Nutmegs, which would look well and be very interesting in your Museum, I could also get you specimens of Many Kinds of Timber but they I fear would be expensive on account of their great weight.

I have been making every inquiry respecting getting some double cocoa-nuts for rearing for you, but as yet I have not been successful, but I make no doubt but I will get them by and by, wee have but one plant here which is about 5 feet high, it is not growing well. I suppose the ground hade not been trenched when it was planted.

I am sory to say wee lost many of the plants you sent the two Palms is however growing. Wee had a very long Passage out 5 months, & when wee got here they lay some time in town before I could get them home, & even when I got them home I had no place to plant them in, I will however be better prepared when you send again, which I hope you will often do, I will return your case full sometime during next summer, before that time I hope to be able to visit the hills and get some of the curious plants. — If you could prevail on Mr Bojer to be a little more communicative he could be of great use to me at Presant, as you may readilly suppose there is many plants here that I am unacquainted with, he is however very distant and very reserved, he has only visited the Gardens once since I came here, & then he would not go round it with me — he appears to me to be a very selfish man. I understand he wished the Gardens to have been sold, and if so, he intended to have purchased them, opened a Hotel and made a sort of Tea Garden of them , but if he felt dissapointed I was not the cause of it — The Public is now however becoming attached to the Garden again and I do not think they would hear of its being sold — I would however be glad if Mr. Bojer would help me for a while as he would enable me to do my duty much better, If not I will send you some dried specimens amongest the plants I am unacquainted with aranged in that way — if you have any Books by you that you can spare that would assist me pray send me them, I have inclosed a slip of paper with the names of a few plants that I think would be very desirable here — but above all see if the Garden cannot be got into better order, & some regulations made as to when and where the Public be admitted, at presant they come in & go out anywhere and at all times, break & destroy everything that comes in their way. The Garden contains about 50 Acres of Land, my presant allowance of men is 19 Malabar Indians, they are paid £1.4.0 each per month — They are a very lazy set of men & very ackward. Many of them never worked till they were brought here. They require to be constantly watched otherwise they will do nothing they are also terrible thieves.

I hope you will excuse my long story and please let me know of the few things I have sent are usefull and what state they reach you in.[4]

The box carried by Captain Smith reached Kew safely, and its contents – including the white ants' nest – were listed in the Entry Book of the Museum of Economic Botany on 12th February, 1851. James was one of the first contributors to what is the magnificent store-house of this Museum, which had been opened just four years earlier.

The sample of the dried fruit of the *Lecythis minor*, or *L. lanceolata*, can be seen in the Museum. With its striking form of a bowl with a lid it is sometimes called the 'monkey pot' – empty pods were filled with bait for monkeys, which inserted their hands and found they could not withdraw their closed fists.[5]

No one from Kew wrote to acknowledge the arrival of this first box of specimens. This disappointed James. However, he continued to look for specimens that might be of interest to Kew, including the 'double cocoa-nuts', by which he undoubtedly meant the coco de mer.

10

'This beautiful and fertile island'

The attitude of the local government to the Pamplemousses garden did not immediately improve. James Duncan's first governor, Sir George Anderson, left Mauritius after only a year in office, and J.M. (later Sir James) Higginson replaced him. So far as the environment in general was concerned, the new governor's attitude can be found in a rather self-satisfied report which he sent to Earl Grey in October 1851.

> I have now completed a tour of the rural districts, during which the favourable impressions that I had been led to form . . . have been amply confirmed. . . . I saw, in some quarters, luxuriant [sugar] canes covering lands redeemed within a few years from the forest or the rock. . . . I will not pretend to estimate the maximum production of sugar of which this fertile soil is capable; that it at present falls far short of that limit is unquestionable. . . . But for clearing forest lands . . . a large accession of capital and labour is required.[1]

There was no doubt in his mind as to the desirability of converting forest to sugar plantation. The adverse ecological effects of deforestation and plantation agriculture were ignored. One can read the despatches of Governor Higginson without coming across any awareness that the French environmentalists in 18th century Mauritius had ever existed. Louis Bouton, later secretary of the Royal Society of Arts and Sciences of Mauritius, gave in 1837 and 1838 a series of lectures arguing for state intervention to ensure forest protection. The lectures were received enthusiastically but sugar planters successfully blocked any action being taken for two decades.[2]

There was not much enthusiasm about the Botanic Garden either. Dr Frederic Mouat from Bengal visited Mauritius early in 1851, and left a brief account of what he called 'the pretty and poetical wilderness called the Botanical Garden'.

The vicinity of the tomb of Paul and Virginia, and the garden itself with its formal walks and straight avenues, dilapidated statue of Flora, and quaint old cumbrous seats, will always be interesting spots to the stranger; but the existing state of what might with comparatively little outlay be rendered a small paradise, is much to be regretted. The present gardener, honest and obliging Mr Duncan, has done his best, and with some success, but he is not a scientific botanist, many highly interesting plants are not identified, and the means at his disposal are not such as to enable him to put it in thorough order.[3]

On 8th November 1851 James was finally driven to write a long letter to the colonial secretary.

Sir

I have the honour to submit for the information of His Excellency the Governor, the following remarks in reference to the report of the Finance Committee No 292 in which the Committee state that they donot consider the use of the Botanical Garden to the Colony commensurate with the expence of its maintenance, and suggesting that an inquery be made into the best means of making it more useful.—

This report has taken me by surprise as I was under the impression in common with many others that the Public generally considered the Botanical Garden of great use to the Colony — but as the Gentlemen composing the above mentioned Committee may not be aware of the extent to which the Botanical Garden is useful as a Nursery for raising young plants for the Colony, (although time and more liberal encouragement would even improve its usefulness in that respect) I may state that during the last 12 months upwards of 16000 plants have been issued from the Garden to the inhabitants of the Colony, as well as a large quantity of seeds.— A number of cases of Plants and of seeds , has also been exchanged with other Colonies.—

So that considering the Garden only in the light of a Nursery for introducing, probagating and distributing plants, and seeds to the inhabitants of the Colony, I think that even in that light alone it must be allowed to be of very great service —

Again it spreads a taste for cultivating plants, and fruits, and consequently for cultivating the soil, which must add considerably to the comforts, the enjoyments, and what is of as much importance the Morals of the inhabitants generally — and I therefor beg to differ from the Gentlemen composing the Finance Committee when they say that its utility to the Colony is not commensurate with the expence of its maintenance. That the inhabitants generally do not think so is evident as they have very generally expressed a wish to me, that the Government would allow a much greater number of [men?] to extend the usefulness and improve the appearance of the Garden. Since I took over charge of it I have opened many new walks and it is now so much frequented by the inhabitants as to be of some importance as a Public Promenade, it being the only place of the kind in the Island.—

With reference to incresing the usefulness of the Garden, I donot well see how it could be done, unless by increasing the number of men employed in it. As continuing to propagate plants for distribution as I have lately done and keeping the ground clean is as much as they can do — In fact I have not been able to supply all the Trees and Plants I have been asked for of late, neither have I been able to comply with a request made to me several times by influential persons to bring vegetables etc to the Exhibitions, for the Gentlemen of the Committee must be aware that what was formerly the Experemental & Kitchen Gardens department of this establishment is now seperated from the Botanical Garden, having been given to the late Mr. Newman, and that I have at present no portion of ground suitable for the cultivation of such things.

The carting of cases of Plants etc etc to and from Port Louis I have hitherto been obliged to do at my own expence which I beg to represent to His Excellency as a great hardship and one that he will be pleased to take into consideration and give me the usual allowance for keeping a Horse, as I am obliged to keep an Animal for the above and other purposes connected with the Garden.—

And if my duties call me from home collecting plants in the Forests or otherways, I respectfully submit that I ought to be allowed travelling expences, or an annual allowance in lieu thereof.—

As to improving the Botanical Garden and consequently making it more useful, I beg to suggest

First, That it ought to be properly fenced inn either by planting a living fence, or by building a wall, the latter would be the best, although the former would be the cheapist, A Gate should also be put up at the entrance with a lodge for a Gatekeeper to live in and a Public Road which now passes through the Garden should be turned again into its former course along one side of the Garden, so that one ring fence should inclose the whole grounds, This road was made through the Garden in consequence of a Bridge on the old road having been carried away during a flood, with the exception of this Bridge the road is otherways in good condition.

Secondly, The Powder Mills Canal which passes through the Garden is all but filled up and requires to be cleaned out, and enlarged, to prevent it from overflowing which it allways does after heavy rains, laying a large portion of the Garden under water, some Ponds of water in the Garden also require cleaning out.—

Thirdly A large portion of the Garden should be cleared of the useless bushes now growing on it, the ground trenched and replanted with a fresh collection of Plants.—

Fourthly A portion might be laid out as a Flower Garden for the cultivation of flowering plants, for which the inhabitants are acquiring a great taste.—

Fifthly, The walk should be gravelled with broken stones, or sand, the former would be the cheapest as the stones could be broken on the spot by the prisoners from the Powder Mills Prison, almost free of expence.

Sixthly Proper regulations are wanted for the admission of Visitors to the Garden and the hours fixed, say from 10 A.M. to 6 P.M. so as to exclude an evil disposed and disorderly set of persons who only come to break and steel, and to annoy the respectable and well disposed portion of the Visitors. In reference to this point I may observe, no person should be allowed to enter, or depart from the Garden but by the one entrance from Pamplemousses Green or Plain, and that the attention of the Police might be called to the Garden, and particularly on Sundays.

Seventhly A Carpanter is much [needed?] for making and reparing Plant Cases as they could be got much cheaper that way than by getting them made. In fact a few cases would cost as much as a Carpanters pay for the year, The timber for the purpose could in a great measure be got from old cases araiving here with Government Stores from England, which are I believe at present sold for a mere trifle, their is also plenty of useless Trees in the Garden that could be sawn up into boards for such purposes.— The Carpanter could find ample employment in this work and in keeping up the buildings, sheds, sharpening the labourers tools etc etc.

Eightly The Plants in the Garden might be numbered and a Catalogue compiled to correspond with the numbers, so that persons by refering to the number of a Plant would at once see its name, its use, and all particulars known respecting it.—

Ware the above suggestions carried out, I submit that they would add very much to the usefulness as well as to the beauty of these Gardens.— It will however I have no doubt readily occur to His Excellency that these improvements cannot be carried out with the means allowed at present, but if properly managed the additional expence would be very trifling — The number of men at present voted by Council for the Botanical Garden is 25 Labourers. Adding to this number the Gatekeeper and Carpanter, and the regular assistance of a band of prisoners from the Powder Mills Prison, the extra expence for labour would be only that of two men — And though with this small additional assistance the work would not proceed very rapidly it would however advance progressively and surely, and in a few years I have no doubt the Garden would not only be as now a place of recreation and a nursery for the inhabitants of the Colony, but become better known and appreciated abroad and tend considerably to enrich the Vegetable resources of this beautiful and fertile Island.

I have the honor to be
Sir

Your most Obedient Humble Servant

James Duncan

Director of the Botanical Garden[4]

Whether it was this final rhetorical flourish, or the earlier emphasis on how gardening can improve the morals of the population, or the cumulative effect of the bludgeoning point after point, the message was received. James followed up the letter with another assault, written just at the turn of the year, in which he weighs in even more heavily. 'For reasons unknown to me 19 labourers only are employed in the Botanical Garden . . . notwithstanding that the estimates for this . . . provide for 25 labourers.' Given the rapid growth of weeds in the Colony, it was impossible to do justice to the Garden with fewer men than were budgeted. True, prisoners were sent daily, 'but these men are perfectly useless for Gardening purposes.'[5]

This letter, although signed by James, was written in a different hand, perhaps Sarah's. Maybe he had retired to his bed in frustration or exhaustion.

However, things now moved so fast, that members of the Finance Committee of the Council of Management under its president, Mr Rawson Rawson, had not only made an early visit to the Garden but had written a full report by 24th January.

The Committee had pleasure in reporting that the Garden had been much improved since Mr Duncan had been in charge of it. Several new walks had been formed, waste spaces cleared, and new or rare plants were being cultivated.

They are therefore desirous of encouraging the Director as far as is consistent with due economy, and are not unwilling, with the evidence of progress before them, to recommend a moderate further outlay on the Garden, so that the Colony may derive greater advantages from the larger amount at present expended annually on its maintenance.[6]

The Committee went on in a helpful and constructive way to recommend to the governor virtually all the requests made by James in his letter, even to the extent of recommending a non-pensionable expenses allowance for him of £50 a year. By no means all the recommendations were subsequently allowed, and it took ten years effectively to fulfil all the objectives. However, this Report marks a turning point in the colonial government's relationship with the Botanic Garden for which it was responsible.

11

COLLECTING PLANTS

Two months after the Finance Committee Report was issued, James wrote to Sir William Hooker. He headed the letter 'Royal Botanical Gardens', instead of 'Royal Botanic Garden', a form he was always to use from now on. He told Sir William about his plans for the Garden, and confirmed that he had started sending seeds and plants of what might be interesting species back to Kew.

March 27th. 1852

Sir William

I avail myself of the favourable opportunity of sending you some seeds by the Honourable William Foster Esq. who is about to leave this Colony for England, he has resided in this Colony for about 30 years — he will be able to tell you all particulars respecting the Mauritius in general, as well as about the Botanical Garden — I am now beginning to feel my way a little here, when I first araived a great number of the plants were strangers to me, and another thing I didnot understand the Language comonly spoken, it is a sort of broken French called Creole.

I can however now jabber away a good deal in that way — At the time I araived here the Botanical Garden was very unpopular, The Public complained that they could get no plants from it and that it was so badly kept that it was not worth coming to see, consequently Government would do nothing for it.

I therefore thought that if I could supply the wants of the Public with plants & Trees I might somewhat redeem the good name of the Garden, and if I could do this I should be likely to get some more assistance from Government, in this I have not been dissapointed, the Council have latley voted 6 additional Indians for the Garden, I have not got them yet but I expect to get them next month. I have also got a band of Prisoners from a neighbouring prison to assist with some of [. . .] to get the Garden inclosed and also to erect a gate at the entrance, with a Porter to take charge of it, both of which the Council have agreed should be done. I also requested to get a road stoped which passes through the middle of the Garden, and to reopen an old road which passed along one side of the Garden which would be equally convenient for the Public but would require an outlay of about £200 to build a Bridge which the Government is unwilling to incur at presant, this part of my request is therefor postponed for the present which I am sory for as it would have been a great improvement to the Garden. During the last year I distributed upwards of 16000 plants & Trees, and this year I think wee will much exceed that number.

I assure you I work much harder than I ever did in England, all the Labourers I have got are what is called in England Coolies from India (wee call them Malabars here).

My forman is a coloured man a native of the place but a man of no education whatever, he is however a very steady man and therefor well adapted for keeping the Malabars at their work, but all particular kinds of jobs I must allways be at myself, and being out all day in this Tropical sun I assure you is no joke. I sent you a few things in a box last year but have never heard from you since.

I have the honor to be, etc

James Duncan[1]

Ten days later, he sent more plants to Hooker, this time three cases on board the *Oriental Queen*. He was anxious that someone should be appointed to look out for the shipment. 'I need not tell you as you will be aware many of the plants I now send you is very scarce, at the time I came here only one plant existed in this Island of several of them, I shall be glad to hear that they reach Kew safely and do well.' It seems that Kew was being dilatory in responding.

I have been long expecting to receive some things from you as a young man named Massey a sailor called on me sometime and told me he saw some cases preparing for me in Kew Garden before he left London, I however am sory to say I have never heard anything more about them, I would have been glade if they hade araived and I should have then got the cases for these plants I now send you, I have a great difficulty in getting cases here.—

I sent you a few things in a box last year, but never heard if they reached you or not, it is true they were not of much importance but I hade to make plants before I could send them.—

You will perhaps laugh at my pots, but necessity people say is the mother of invention, when I came here I hadnot got a single garden pot, nor would the Government give me any for a long time so I set to work and made Bambo pots, and they are much better than small clay pots for hot climates as they do not absorb the heat so much — I hope to have the pleasure of receiving many fine things from you before long amongst others, Amherstia Nobilis, & Victoria Regina, and many other fine plants from South America, The West cost of Africa, The West Indies, & Borneo, all Tropical plants will grow well here. —

Hopeing to hear from you soon.[2]

'Victoria regina' is the Amazon water-lily (now *V. amazonica*), much admired by Queen Victoria when shown it at Kew in 1848. It seems likely that James saw it the following year, during his visit to Kew before sailing. Hooker sent James some seeds, from which he raised three plants, one of which was showing flowers, when an accident occurred. James reported in a letter of 1855 that the plants were growing in a pond containing other water-lilies, the roots of which some of the Indian gardeners treated as a delicacy. 'One day one of them paid my pond a visit — and in addition to carying away the Nymphas pulled out and destroyed all the Victorias, I must therefor beg of you to send me a further supply of seeds.'[3] The plant now grows abundantly in the centre of the Pamplemousses Botanic Garden, where the Lily Pond is one of the most popular attractions.

Two of the boxes sent to Kew contained 41 plants, annotated on the contents list with comments by James which show clearly his enthusiasm for this new flora, of which he had had experience for only two years: '*Aganosma Caryophyllata*, a beautiful climber it is at this present time covered with its beautiful white scented flowers . . . . *Borassus Madagascariensis*, this is a very curious palm when all the trunk is covered with threads like Horse Hair . . . . *Sandoricum Indicum*, a very fine Tree with yellow fruit something like an orange very beautiful but very sour, not at all pleasant to eat,' and so on.

The third case contained tree ferns, and he provided an account of how he collected these.

Case marked D7 and adressed as before is intirely filled with Cryptogamous plants from the Forests here. It contains three plants of Tree Ferns one of which is as large as I could put into the case. I was a longtime before I could succeed in getting one to grow this large, one I have hade at Pamplemousses for three months and at the time I put it into the case it had abundance of young roots which it have made since I brought it home.

They only grow on the Mountains where the climate is very damp about 24 miles from Pamplemousses and up hill nearly all the way. I was however very anxious to get some of these plants to send you so I hired a carrage for the purpose which cost £3 for the day and collected as many things as I could carry home with me but many of them died afterwards I now send you all the Tree ferns that survived.

When one first sees these plants they have no idea that they are Ferns as at a little distance they look like Palm Trees many of them are 10 & 15 feet high. It is however a very difficult task to go far into these places as one soon looses their way and with a Tropical sun pouring his rays like a lense on ones head climbing amongest Rocks & Roots and jumping over water soon compels a person to think of reatracing their steps back again.

I have no doubt but thare is many kinds of Plants in these Forests as yet unknown to Science.

It was not only to Kew that James was now sending plants. In 1852 he despatched a case of seeds to Calcutta for the Agri-Horticultural Society of the Punjab. There is also a good record of plant exchanges with Sydney. The new director of the Botanic Gardens there, Charles Moore – also, as it happens, appointed by Earl Grey on the advice of John Lindley – produced from 1850 onwards detailed annual reports of exchanges with other gardens. In 1851, for example, Pamplemousses sent 20 specimens to Sydney, and 24 were sent in return to 'Mr Duncan, Botanic Gardens, Mauritius'.[4] These included palms, ferns, cycads and orchids, as well as Australian trees like the Norfolk Island pine and the Moreton Bay chestnut. Pamplemousses had become part of the network of nineteenth century botanic gardens distributing rare, beautiful, or economically useful plants world wide.

There were plant exchanges also with Ferdinand von Mueller, the remarkable director of the Melbourne Botanic Garden (he must be the only director of a botanic garden about whom an opera has been written.)[5] Unfortunately, much of Mueller's correspondence has been destroyed, but even so a large number of his letters have been located and have recently been published. In 1853, his first report as Government Botanist in Victoria 'set out the four-fold purpose of a botanic garden as he saw it – education, acclimatization of foreign plants, research on native plants, and healthy recreation for the citizenry.'[6]

It was not uncommon for directors of botanic gardens who were botanists to fall into dispute with their committees of management who were less concerned with taxonomy and botanical science in general than with the physical attractiveness of the gardens and the supply of plants to local residents; and this was the eventual fate of Ferdinand von Mueller. In the case of Mauritius, James Duncan, being a gardener and not a botanist, was less likely to have problems of this kind, and in any case the Report of 1852 firmly established economic botany as the main priority:

It must be borne in mind that the principal object of this institution is to introduce, propagate, and distribute useful plants, and that the dressing of the borders for the purpose of affording an agreeable promenade to visitors is a matter which should be kept secondary to the chief end.[7]

James was quite happy to accept this main objective. The year after the Report was issued, he wrote to Kew asking particularly for 'plants from Tropical countries and above all Tropical fruits and Medical plants.'[8] Then, in 1855, he wrote to Kew on the subject of paper.

I have lately received from Calcutta a plant of the Aralia papyrifera which the Chinese rice paper is said to be made from. . . . Have you got the Urtica nivea the fibre of which the beautiful grass cloth is made from. If not, I can send it to you as I have a fine batch of it here, it is a native plant.

I hear of a great scarcity of materials to make paper from. I should think the trash from the Sugar Mills would answer well (I mean the sugar cane after the juice has been crushed out of) and if so it could be hade in any quantity in every Colony where the Sugar Cane is grown.[9]

As time went on, James did regret that more scientific work could not be done locally. For example, there was no herbarium at Pamplemousses during his time there.

His letters to Hooker now became more personal. On 1st February 1853, he sent him a box containing some specimens for the Kew Museum with, in addition – marked private – two gifts, a card basket and a pin cushion, both made from local seeds. 'The former was made by my son and the latter by my daughter for you. The basket will no doubt be much out of shape when it reaches you but you can easily bend it into its proper shape.' One of the plants being sent was of special interest.

Amongst the specimens for your Museum is a branch of Flacourtia Ramontchi a plant which I have commenced fencing in the Botanic Garden with it is a most splendid plant for making hedges with I think superior to the thorn of England. The specimen will show you what kind of fence it will make.[10]

This was the Madagascar plum, a tree of which it was said that, thanks to its formidable thorns, it formed hedges which made such an impenetrable barrier, that even chickens could not get through. Other useful plants included *Bambusa spinosa* which James had been told was used in Burma to form stockades which were impenetrable, and part of a leaf stalk of the palm *Sagus Ruffia*, which was used in Mauritius to form rafters and ladders. 'They are allmost imperishable & no insects will touch them the out side being nearly as hard as Bone.'

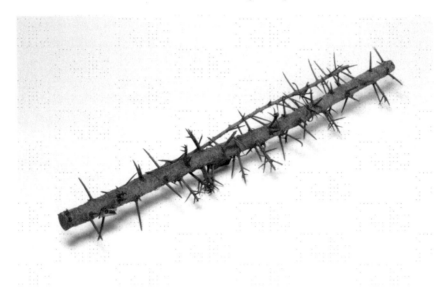

The branch of the Madagascar plum can still be seen, beautifully preserved, in the Museum of Economic Botany at Kew. It has spiny thorns as sharp as they were described a hundred and fifty years ago.

Another object still to be seen at Kew is the dried fruit of a *Luffa acutangula*, 'a vegetable very much used in Mauritius', according to James, and close relative of our bathroom loofah. It is a versatile plant, as shown by its common names, Chinese okra or vegetable sponge: when young, it is cooked as a vegetable, while the fibrous netting of older and dried fruits make an excellent sponge, or even a water filter.[11]

Two months later, James sent Sir William another case of plants. This time he also mentioned plants he would like in return. (Mr Smith was John Smith, the curator at Kew.)

> I wrote to Mr. Smith about two months since and gave him a list of a number of plants that I should like to have providing you have them to spare, and I hope I give you some evidence of my willingness to serve you. . . . I am getting this garden into a little better order although it is yet very far from what I would like it to be. I am at presant making a large pond and will be glade of all the beautiful acquatics you can send me, I should think they would come well in vials of water amongst the soil in the cases. I have lately got some seeds of Nelumbium Speciosum from India. It was formerly grown here but during the time the Garden was so neglected it as well as many other things was lost.[12]

The seeds James had received from India were those of the sacred lotus. He went on to report that he was making a collection of ferns, and another of orchids, one of which bore a flower 'very like the Lilly of the Valley, and quite as sweet-scented perhaps it is a Dendrobium, it might well be called the Lilly of the Valley of Mauritius'.

However, not everything was positive.

> I am very fond of exploring the woods but with my small income I cannot afford to go very often in this expensive place. Beef such as you would give to your Dogs is selling at from 1/- to 1/3d per lb. Mutton much higher and very poor, Salt pork 1/- per lb. Flour varies in price from 5d to 10d per lb and all other things in proportion, so that you may easily conceive keeping a family here on my income is no joke — and this is not all. Schooling is very expensive. I have two fine Boys will soon be men and what to do with them I cannot tell, nearly every Government situation here is filled by the Creoles whom our present Governor appears very anxious to conciliate.
>
> Since I have been here I hade one very serious attack of fever otherways my health has generally been good. I am however sory to say my wife enjoys

very bad health, she is laid up at present, indeed I may say she is never well of late.

The Hot Season is very trying here and our houses having no fire places in them when the wet weather set in everything soon becomes very damp and we have no means of drying anything till the sun shines again, consequently our Beds as well as our clothing all becomes quite damp. Tropical Countrys are very interesting to visit for a short time but only a very few Europeans that can stand them long.

The following year came a crisis for the whole island – an epidemic of cholera, brought in from India. There were 200 deaths a day in Port Louis, 60 in Pamplemousses. The cause of cholera was still not understood, though any number of potential treatments were recommended – such as sulphuric acid and cold douches. The epidemic came close to James's family. 'Two of my sons had attacks, Thank God but slight they are now quite well again.'[13] The family was growing up. 'My two oldest Boys are now nearly as tall as myself, they will be able to leave School in another year. . . . They are fine steady Boys.'[14] However, the sickness was hard to shake off. In November, he wrote:

I have had my oldest Son very ill for some time past, poor fellow I fear he caught cold while ranging the forests after plants & he has been laid up with fever for nearly two months, but I am glade to say he is now a little better and begins to walk a little again.[15]

James's own health also suffered.

I think I have preaviously told you that I was obliged to ride in an open conveyance, since I last wrote to you I was suddenly taken ill while from home, fortunately some persons were near who hade me sent home in a carriage. The Doctor atributed it to a stroke of the Sun and tells me I must be more careful for the future.[16]

Apart from issues of health, James wrote frequently on the subject of money, or rather the lack of it. Mauritius was certainly an expensive place in which to live. The Revd Patrick Beaton, minister of St Andrew's church and secretary of the Bible Society of Mauritius, wrote: 'No one can know how dear living is in this colony till he has tried the experiment. . . A colonial chaplain, with £400 a-year, finds it difficult to live on his salary.'[17] The government in Port Louis and the

Colonial Office in London tossed the subject of salaries in the Botanic Garden to and fro, and James wrote frequently to Sir William Hooker asking him for help, including suggestions for pulling down favours:

> I would advise you to see Sir George Grey on the Subject, he knows me well, I fought hard for him during the Northumberland election & I think he is a favour in my debt. . . . [18]

To what benefit this suggestion was made is unclear, since Hooker too was involved in a balancing act between salaries at Kew and those in the increasing number of gardens overseas.

In any event, James did not give up on the subject of his salary. He pointed out that on £250 a year he could not afford to pay for a covered vehicle, essential under the tropical sun, the absence of which he blamed for his sunstroke. Eventually, he reported to Hooker that although he had not had a salary increase, he had been voted a £50 allowance, which he described as 'miserable'. It may have been frustration over his salary that lay behind the ironic tone of a letter sent to the colonial secretary in Port Louis in August 1855:

> Sir
>
> In order to destroy a species of insect which has infected many of the Trees & Shrubs here, I have lately cut down some useless bushes of sappan which were covered with it, to try and prevent its spreading — The above mentioned sappan being growing near a small stream of water I am told that according to Ordinance No 30 of 1854 I have rendered myself liable to a penalty of £10.
>
> There being so many small streams of water in the Botanical Garden, it would be impossable to carry out the improvements there without often coming within the strict letter of this Ordinance, for instance, I intended commencing soon to enclose the Garden on the East side by planting a living fence, but in order to accomplish this I must first clear and trench the ground, and as there is a small stream of water within 50 feet, here I should again be liable to be prosecuted although done with the intention of replanting the ground.
>
> In all cases where I clear away useless jungle here it is only done to make room for more useful plants, or for plants new to the Colony, and which will again serve the purpose of shading the streams of water.

I cannot for a moment believe that the above Ordinance was ever intended to prevent such improvements from being carried out here.

I will therefore feel obliged by your moving His Excellency the Governor, that the Botanical Garden be exempted from the operation of the above mentioned Ordinance, viz No 30 of 1854.[19]

There is no record of the colonial secretary's response.

In spite of these frustrations, this period represents a fulfilment of James's aims, when a visit to Pamplemousses became an essential part of every tourist's stay in Mauritius; though these same visitors also caused him difficulties.

Persons out under a Tropical Sun even if they ride in a Carrage soon require some refreshment in the way of drink at least, consequently they apply to me & I cannot refuse them when I see them ready to faint, and believe me this alone is a very heavy tax upon me.[20]

12

'The kind and obliging gardener'

Tourism was well established in the mid-nineteenth century, and when visitors travelled in Mauritius, they went to see the Botanic Garden. Many – including numerous clergymen – left records of their visits.

One of these was the Revd Patrick Beaton, mentioned earlier. He was a sabbatarian, though he did, in addition, have a wry sense of humour. When he first arrived on the island he was struck by how the Sabbath was ignored, everyone either working or 'hurrying to the country to spend the Sabbath at Pamplemousses'. So in due course, he followed the crowds out to the Botanic Garden.

> While the term botanical is rather misapplied to these gardens, they are interesting from the collection of trees, shrubs and herbaceous plants, peculiar to the tropics, which they contain. Among the plants are some magnificent sago palms, and an interesting collection of spice-growing trees and shrubs. The nutmeg tree is generally an object of great interest to travellers. Its fruit resembles a Green Chissel pear, and when it is ripe, it bursts open and exposes to view the nutmeg, covered with its coating of bright red mace. Mr Duncan, the kind and obliging gardener, is ever ready to supply travellers with specimens of the nutmeg, which, when preserved in brine, form an interesting souvenir of Mauritius. A specimen of the mangoustan tree, the fruit of which is regarded as superior to every other, may also be seen; but owing to the difference of soil and climate between Mauritius and Malacca, from which it was brought, the fruit never reaches maturity. Mr Duncan has made an extensive collection of the ferns indigenous to the island, and the traveller will never regret a day spent amid the fine shady alleys and tropical exuberance of Pamplemousses Gardens.[1]

Not long afterwards, the gardens were visited by the first Anglican bishop of Mauritius, Vincent Ryan. He had been appointed in 1854, and was consecrated at Lambeth simultaneously with the Bishop of Sydney. Before leaving for his new diocese, he collected funds of over £1,000, of which £200 came from the 'venerable dowager Lady Grey', that is, the second earl's widow. It would seem that the Grey family were maintaining their interest in the island. The bishop arrived in Port Louis in June 1855, and a fortnight later paid a visit to Pamplemousses.

PETER-BOTTE.

Wednesday, June 27th. – Captain West, the proprietor of the estate at Grand Bay, called for me at 10 A.M., and I started with him in his carriage, accompanied by Mr. Weston, to look at the schools, as I had promised. The morning had been showery, so that the air was very refreshing, and even cool. We stopped at Pamplemousses, about seven miles from Port Louis, to go over the famous Botanical Gardens there. Mr. Duncan, who has charge of them, was very cordial in welcoming me to the island, and seemed really glad for himself and others at the prospect of a service on Sundays. The trees in the garden were very fine – many kinds of palm, the cinnamon, the clove-tree, the nutmeg, the bamboo, especially the thorny bamboo, gave the place a thoroughly oriental appearance. It was with strange feelings that I looked upon these fine specimens of a vegetation hitherto known to me only by books or in conservatories. From the top of a long avenue of palms the summit of Pieter Botte could be seen through the vista, and the effect was very fine. What would some of our friends in England give for such a sight! Not far from the gardens we saw the site of the new church which is to erected, and for which a subscription has been begun in the village of Pamplemousses.[2]

There was already a church opposite the main entrance of the Botanic Garden, the large Roman Catholic church of St Francis of Assisi, the oldest on the island. There was also a Presbyterian 'Scots Church' in Port Louis. James's own religious beliefs are hard to establish, but would appear to have been moderate. It is likely, but by no means certain, that he was an Episcopalian in upbringing. His reading might have included the three best-selling books of the second quarter of the 19th century, the Bible, *The Pilgrim's Progress*, and *Robinson Crusoe*.

The petition for a Protestant church at Pamplemousses had been signed in 1851 by James Duncan, along with other British residents, named George Ireland, H.M. Self, Reilly, and N. Noble.[3] Lady Higginson, the governor's wife, was to lay the foundation stone in 1857, and the church of St Barnabas was opened in 1859. It was located not far from the side entrance into the Garden which led to the director's house.

Another ecclesiastical visitor (and an early photographer) was the Revd William Ellis, who attended the annual exhibition of agriculture, arts and sciences in September 1853. He was impressed by the flower show. 'One of the most gorgeous plants was an *Alpinia magnifica* [a ginger], from the royal gardens at Pamplemousses, on which the bunch or cone of scarlet flowers rose on a stalk eight or ten feet from the ground. There was a collection exhibited by Mr Duncan of fifty sorts of roses and some fragrant and beautiful violets.' We will return to these roses later. Meanwhile, Ellis was in Pamplemousses again early the following year.

I had more than once visited them before, when I had been highly gratified by the kind attentions of Mr Duncan, the director, and the members of his family, from whom I again received a frank and hearty welcome, with the offer of such accommodation as they could furnish for my photographic operations.

So far as natural objects were concerned, no place in Mauritius was to me so attractive as the Royal Gardens at Pamplemouses [sic]. They cover about fifty acres of most excellent ground, and are well supplied with water. They appear to have been originally laid out on a truly magnificent scale. Long walks or avenues, with stone seats at intervals on both sides, are bordered with the most rare and valuable trees of both hemispheres, interspersed with an almost endless variety of shrubs and flowers. Many improvements in the arrangement of some portions of the grounds were in progress; and the whole seemed to be kept in as good order as the number of labourers assigned to them were capable of maintaining. Many of the useful trees and plants of Europe may be found here; and the number of choice roses recently introduced by Mr Duncan adds greatly to the charm and attractions of the place. But the gardens are especially rich in the productions of China, India, and the Asiatic Archipelago. Some of the most choice specimens are from Java and the adjacent islands, while there are others from the continent of Africa, as well as from Australia and South America. There is one noble avenue of palmists, or palms; it is at least four hundred yards in length, and for extent and beauty is probably unequalled in any other part of the globe. The trees are remarkably regular on both sides, presenting few openings or chasms. The tallest are forty or fifty feet high, and have probably been growing where they now stand for nearly a century. The young trees, more recently planted, nearer the centre of the walk, cover the lower parts of the trunks of the palms, and add greatly to the graceful beauty of the vista, along which the lines of lofty waving plumes extend. . . .

Almost every variety of the palm species, or form of growth, is to be found in these gardens, and I was much struck with the graceful slender forms of some beautiful arecas. There were also fine specimens of the *Latania rubra*, or fan-leaved palm, and the singular leaved *Caryota urens*, the rofia tree, the traveller's tree, and *Dombeya cuspidata*, the last three from Madagascar, as were also many of the rare and curious plants in different parts of the grounds. There were some large trees of Adansonia [the baobab], and hibiscus with flowers of almost every hue, growing luxuriantly, and requiring scarcely any other care than to be kept within bounds by the pruning knife.[4]

Ellis was a contributor to the Garden himself, presenting James with a specimen of the aquatic plant *Ouvirandra* (now *Aponogeton*) *fenestrale* which he had collected in Madagascar following the advice of Dr Bojer as to its location.

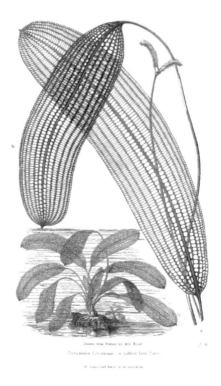

Perhaps the most remarkable account by a visitor at that period was that of the Austrian traveller and writer Ida Pfeiffer, who was born in Vienna in 1797. She had two sons, and when the boys had grown up, she embarked on a series of major journeys. Her first was to Palestine: her account of the trip was successful, and brought her enough money to finance a journey round northern

Europe, followed by two round world tours, the book resulting from each tour financing the next one. In May 1856 she set out yet again, this time to the Indian Ocean, and she landed in Mauritius in December.

Her account of the island and the way of life of its inhabitants at that time is frequently caustic but always lively. This is how she began her tour of the island:

First of all, I visited the town of Port Louis. There was little enough to be seen in it. Though of tolerable size (it has a population of 50,000), it possesses not a single fine public building, with the exception of the Government-house and the bazaar. . . . The bridge across the big river – frequently so destitute of water that it can be easily forded – is built tastefully enough, only they have been so sparing of its breadth that only one carriage can go across it at a time; when two meet, one has to wait till the other has passed. Governments seem to act very much like private people: so long as they have little money, or, indeed, are in debt, they are generous, and even extravagant; but from the moment when they become prosperous they grow saving and avaricious. At least, this seems to be the case with the Government of the Mauritius, which is much more stingy, with its well-filled chest, than our European States that are burdened with debt. Does it not show a miserable want of spirit, to have such a narrow bridge in the busiest part of the town?

Two other bridges, of hewn stone, fairly fell in during my stay; fortunately, no one was hurt. Each Governor thinks only of filling the treasury; his greatest pride is in being able to say, that under his rule the surplus of income over expenditure had increased by so many thousand pounds. Acting on this principle, the present Governor objected strongly to the estimates given in for the building of the two bridges, ordered that they should be constructed at a cheaper rate, and — has the pleasure of building them twice over.

Ida Pfeiffer next turned her eye towards the social customs among the European residents.

At sunrise we refreshed ourselves with a cup of coffee, brought into the bedroom; between nine and ten the bell summoned us to a breakfast of rice, curry and a few hot dishes; and at one came a luncheon of fruit or bread-and-cheese. The chief meal was taken in the evening, generally after seven o'clock. . . .

Social intercourse does not flourish in the Mauritius. There is not even a club here; the chief reason may be that the society consists of French and English in almost equal numbers, — two nations whose characters and modes of thinking vary too much ever to amalgamate freely.

Besides this chief obstacle, there are other minor hindrances: for instance, the late dinner-hour, and the great distances between the various houses. As I have observed, the usual dinner-hour is between seven and eight o'clock, and thus the whole evening is lost. In other hot countries, when it is customary for people to live in country houses outside the town, the gentlemen generally come home from their business at five o'clock, and dine at six, so that at seven people are ready to receive visitors and friends.

But here all visits are paid before dinner, as it is too late to do so afterwards, and whoever wants to assemble a few people for the evening, must invite them solemnly to dinner. These dinners are conducted with great ceremony. Every one appears in full dress, the officials generally in uniform, as if they had received an invitation to Court. At table, one is frequently seated between two perfect strangers, and after suffering the horrors of ennui for hours, a move is made at past nine o'clock into the reception-rooms, there to suffer ennui for some time longer. Music is very seldom introduced. Packs of cards are everywhere displayed on the tables, but I never saw them used. Every guest seems to be waiting with impatience for the time when he may take his leave without appearing rude; he is devoutly thankful when the evening has come to an end, and then accepts the next invitation with the greatest pleasure.

Still, Ida Pfeiffer was entertained by a few congenial hosts; and in due course she made her way to Pamplemousses.

I would not quit the district of Pamplemousses without visiting the Botanical Garden, which is under the superintendence of the accomplished botanist and director, Mr. Duncan.

Scarcely had I spent a quarter of an hour with this amiable man, a Scotchman by birth, before he invited me, in the most friendly manner, to spend a few days in his house, that I might be able to examine the treasures of the garden at my leisure. Though I had become somewhat careful in the matter of Mauritian invitations, I could not resist the real good nature of Mr. Duncan. I stayed with him, and had no cause to repent it. Mr. Duncan was a man of few words, but he did what he could to make my residence in his house agreeable. When he saw that I was collecting insects, he himself helped me in my search, and often brought me some new specimens for my collection.

I walked several times with him through the Botanical Garden, which is very rich in plants and trees from all parts of the world. Here I saw for the first time trees and shrubs from Madagascar, indigenous to that island. I particularly admired a water-plant, the *Hydrogiton fenestralis* [sic], whose leaves, three inches in length and one in breadth, are quite pierced through, as if by artificial means pieces had been broken out. A tree, the *Adansonea digitata* [sic], is remarkable, not for its beauty, but for its ugliness. The stem is of uniform clumsy thickness to a height of eight or ten feet; then it becomes suddenly thin: the bark is of a light unsightly colour, quite smooth and almost shining.

There were many spice-trees, and a few specimens of the beautiful water-palm, which I have already seen and described in my "Second Voyage round the World".

I am no botanist, and can therefore give no detailed description of the garden; but competent persons have assured me that it is very judiciously and scientifically laid out. To look at the varied and numerous plants, and the extensive plantations, sometimes requiring great labour to cultivate, no one would believe that Mr. Duncan has very restricted resources at his command. The Government only allows him twenty-five labourers, Malabars and Bengalees, who certainly do not get through as much work as eight or ten strong Europeans would accomplish.[5]

Presumably the last remark was suggested to her by James. Who else could make the comparison between garden labourers in Europe and those in Mauritius?

The government did eventually relent, though not very much. In the year that James left Mauritius there were thirty unnamed labourers on the establishment, along with five named individuals and the director himself: the head gardener (John Horne), the overseer (William Stephens), the guardian (John Robert Hutchinson), the carpenter (Renée), and the mason (Théophile).[6]

13

THE FAMILY

Shortly after Ida Pfeiffer's visit, James and Sarah suffered a heartbreaking loss.

8th May 1857

Sir William

I am sory to have the painfull duty of informing you of the loss of my youngest son, he died of Fever on the 15th of March. He complained of pains in his limbs & on that day week he was a corpse. He was a fine promising youth 18 years of age universally respected by all who knew him, he had just finished his education and left College about three weeks. He was a youth particularly fond Science particularly of Botany & Natural History so much so that he was often called the Young Naturalist. Had he lived he intended to have made drawings of all the plants in Mauritius so that a new Catalogue might have been made from them. He has left upwards of 400 drawings of plants all taken from nature he has also left the finest Collection of native insects that has ever been made all collected by himself. His sudden death was a great shock to us all. . . .

The present hot season has lasted for an unusually long time and consequently sickness has been very general — the nights are now beginning to get a little cooler & I can assure you wee all stand much in need of a change of climate. Our Governor leaves us soon and although he lives in the coolest part of the Island his health is by no means good. The Colony has been very prosperous under his Administration principally owing to the high price of sugar.[1]

The exact date of Ida Pfeiffer's visit is not known, but it was certainly no more than a few weeks before young George's death. It is curious that she makes no mention of James's family at all in her book, even though she does write about how James himself helped her with her collection of insects, and how she was invited to stay in his house. Surely she must have been shown George's collection? One also wonders what happened to the collection of drawings. It was certainly large, four times as big as that which George's elder brother James William presented to Kew in 1894. Can all those botanical illustrations really have been destroyed at some point during the past 150 years? Perhaps they will turn up one day.

There was, however, positive news for James to pass on to Hooker at the same time. In a separate letter, he wrote that both his surviving sons now had jobs.[2] James William (nearly 22) was an assistant draughtsman in the Survey

Department, while John Corbett (two years younger) was a clerk in the colonial secretary's office. Each had an annual salary of £100.

The National Archives of Mauritius still contain one of James William's early plans. It shows the village of Pamplemousses and a corner of the Botanic Garden as they were in 1859, but is in poor condition and difficult to read. The Protestant church had just been built, and the public road still ran across the Garden, as a result of its original route having been blocked by the collapse of the bridge across the river. Curiously, 'Le Petit Jardin', the corner of the Garden cut off from the rest by a road and the river, is left blank on the map, leaving the question of whether that definitely was the site of the director's house uncertain. There is no indication, either, of the Bridge of Sighs which today crosses the river and links the two parts of the Garden, leaving open the possibility that James had it built between 1859 and his departure from Mauritius. However, it is more likely that it was built by John Newman after he bought the new land in 1829, in order to link what subsequently became the two parts of the Botanic Garden.[3]

A year after George's death, there was a big family celebration. On 25th February 1858, civil marriages took place at Pamplemousses (the Protestant church was not yet open) of two of James' and Sarah's children, John Corbett and his sister Caroline. John Corbett had met his wife on a visit to South Africa: her name was Frances Maria McDougal, and she had been born in the Cape of Good Hope to a Scottish father. Caroline's husband was named Hubert James Coombs. One of six children born to James and Sarah Coombs (or Coombes), he was living in Port Louis, where presumably Caroline now moved. There was one child from their marriage, a daughter named Lilly, but when Caroline's parents returned to Britain from Mauritius, she followed them soon after, leaving Hubert in Port Louis, where he died in 1870.

The other bride, Frances Maria, gave birth to twins just nine months after the wedding. Named Charlotte Sarah and John Frances James, they were born half an hour apart on the afternoon of 31st October. But life was fragile in the nineteenth century tropics, and the baby boy died just three days after birth. (Rather confusingly, he is named John Frances on his birth certificate, but John James on his death certificate, perhaps because the registrar accepted only two forenames.) Other children followed: George was born in 1860, and Caroline in 1862, both in Pamplemousses.

Meanwhile, James occupied himself with his work. He had two problems to deal with: firstly a white insect that had made its appearance on the island and which was destroying valuable plants; and secondly he needed to devise a way of shipping to Kew samples of the large, but delicate, germinating seeds of the coco de mer (*Lodoicea maldivica*). The seed, the largest in the plant kingdom, weighs about 15 kg and can take a year to germinate. Trees do not produce their first flowers until they are over twenty years old.

29th April 1857

Sir William

Having heard that the plant of Lodoicea that the late Mr. Bojer sent you had died I was therefore very anxious to replace it but I was at a great loss to know how I could send them with the seeds attached to them without which I didnot think they would live. I have had a case prepared with the sashes in two halves & by this means I have been able to suspend the seeds in the top of the case. I have just finished it & I hope they will reach you in good condition & do well. You will now see the strange manner in which this plants vegetates from the seed.

I will now take the liberty of offering a few remarks as to the best manner of taking them out of the case without injuring the plants. I will first remark that the roots of this plant are of a very soft fleshy nature and consequently very easily bruised after which they are very lyable to rot. A light sandy soil I think will suit it best but I do not think it is very particular as to soil, they grow well in our Garden here, but of course very slowly as they only make one leaf in a year. There was one plant here before I came it is now about 10 feet high and has not as yet begun to form its trunk being merely a bunch of its enormous leaves.

But I am wandering from my subject viz taking the plants out of the case. First I would recommend the lower halves of the sashes on both sides to be removed this will distend everything then take out all the other plants they are in pots — I would now remove one side of the Box – but be <u>very carefull not to destroy the top halves of the sashes</u>. All the soil may now be carefully taken out without wounding or bruising the roots.

The plants will now be suspended by their seeds from the top of the case in the same way that they ware put in — The nails will now require to be drawn out which keeps the pieces of wood in place on which the seeds rests, supporting the seeds with a hand at the same time to prevent their falling and breaking the plants — let the seeds remain attached to the plants untill they become well established — a Temperature of 80 or 90 will suit these best till they are established.[4]

The timing of this letter is curious. It was written (if the dates at the head of the letters are correct) just over a week *before* James wrote to Sir William Hooker with news of George's death – yet the young man had died two months earlier, in the middle of March. Why was there a delay in writing about his son? Then two weeks later, he wrote again, this time to say that the case containing the coco de mer plants had been put safely on board ship. He went on to write about the insect pest, an interesting example of 'biological control'.

12th May 1857

I am happy to say another insect I think a species of Ladybird has made its appearance here (in just as misterious a manner as the other white one did) that feeds upon it — I send you a few inclosed they will of course be dead before they reach you but you may be able to know something of them even in a dried state — I am now in hopes that wee may ultimatly get rid of this white pest, you can scarcely form an idea of the trouble and anxiety it has given me for upwards of twelve wee have done nothing but try to destroy it by cutting of all the branches from the trees and burning them, at one time I thought every wooded kind of plant in the Island would have been destroyed by them — you may therefore readily conceive how glad we were to find that the bountiful Creator of all things had provided a remedy for us.

You will please let me know in what state the Lodoicea reaches you as I feel very anxious about them Capt. Ritchie has promised me that he will take great care of them.[5]

Perhaps the timely appearance of this ladybird in Mauritius gave extra comfort to James as he dealt with, and partially suppressed, his grief at the death of his son.

14

'... SINCE I BECAME A TROPICAL PLANT MYSELF'

At the beginning of 1857, James paid his first visit to Round Island, and it was perhaps there that his especial interest in palms arose. Round Island lies off the north coast of Mauritius, and today is a barren spot.[1] James's brief seems to have been to investigate the island as a potential economic resource. He reported on the existing trees (coconuts, screw pine, and casuarina) and said that the soil was good. He recommended the planting of tropical fruit trees, shelter belts being established first.[2]

However, after a further visit he described the island as 'allmost a barren rock in the sea' and the landing to be so difficult that it could be approached 'only when the weather is very calm and even then only at certain Seasons of the Year'.

The Island is not far from the main land as we can reach it in a day with a good Boat for which wee pay £5 (but a person may go several times before they can land) & then sleep a night on the Island or in the boat — spend a day on the Island and return during the night — on the Island the heat is most oppresive and no water to be had it swarms with a species of Lissard great beast about a foot long or more and some of them as large as a mans wrist — it is not at all agreeable to sleep among them although they are said to be harmless.[3]

In spite of its small size, Round Island is home to some endemic palms, specimens of which can be seen today in the Pamplemousses Garden. They include the blue latan (*Latania loddigesii*) and the palmiste gargoulette (*Hyophorbe lagenicaulis*), both introduced to the Garden by James.[4]

I have spent a deal of money visiting our Dependencies and forests searching out these new Palms and incured dangers [on] several Occasions but I have become a great admirer of that splendid and usefull tribe of plants since I became a Tropical plant myself, and I have the gratification of knowing that I have brought many of them into notice which were previously unknown.

Our Garden is particularly well adapted for growing Palms and being large (about 50 Acres) wee could therefor grow one of the finest collections in the world the only draw back is the Huricanes which often breaks them down or tears them up by the root — I am collecting all I can from every quarter and I hope you [Sir William Hooker] will assist me all you can to make our collection as complet as possable. I am expecting a considerable number soon from South Amereca & Java.[3]

'Every quarter' evidently included the Seychelles. A magistrate in Mahe named Charles Telfair, nephew of the Mauritius naturalist of the same name, wrote to Louis Bouton in July 1858 about 'our friend Mr Duncan [of] the Queens Garden'. '[He] presses me much for seeds of the palms from all of the islands, but hitherto I have been unable to get a pinnace for hire to take me to one of them, although I offered $20 for the day.'[5]

James had earlier expressed his growing enthusiasm for palms in another letter to Hooker.

In the Botanical Garden here is a splendid alley of Palm Trees about 1000 yards in length — they are all called Palmists here and people think there is only one or two kinds amongst them, although to a general observer they appear very much alike yet when they are more closely examined there is a great difference in them of appearance, and these seeds differ greatly in size, shape, & colour, some being small, others oblong, whilst others are nearly round, some are green others blue, and some black, some are hard & dry nothing but a skin covering the seed, whilst others are quite pulpy and soft — I have therefor no doubt but there is many kinds amongest them, & I have therefor selected seeds from 24 of them which appears to be as many different kinds; in the dry state in which they will reach you the differance of colour will not be seen, you will however see there is a very great differance in size & shape. I have also sent you seeds of Areca Alba, I donot know whether you have preaviously got it — I have also sent you a few seeds of Stephanotis floribunda it seeds freely here in fact the plants look like a fruit tree covered with their large mango looking seedpods, many people think it must be different kind from the plant grown in Europe under the same name, you can grow a plant or two & see if there is any differances.[6]

There is no single palm lined avenue in the Garden today measuring 1000 yards in length: 300 metres is about the limit, though most of the existing avenues are lined with palms, and they represent perhaps the most characteristic feature of the Pamplemousses Garden. The great avenue of mixed palms referred to in this letter was perhaps destroyed in the great cyclone of 1892.

In addition to Round Island, James saw for himself the much larger Mauritian dependency, the 'beautiful little island', of Rodrigues.

. . . It is about 15 miles long and about 5 broad, the Climate is delightful although in a warmer latitude than Mauritius it is so well tempered by the trade winds that the heat is not at all oppresive — I spent eight days there and travelled over every part of the Island, & collected seeds of every plant that I could find in seed and of [those] I could not get seeds off I brought young plants — the little Case is intirely filled with plants from that Island & the Pandanus in the large Case is also from there.

I found three new Palms No 1 I have called Latania Aurea the other species of this fine family being known by their different colours, this one is of a fine golden yellow it is a <u>true Latania</u> (I will send you a specimen of its seeds) [it is] a noble plant & certainly the most useful plant to the inhabitants that the Island produces.—

No 8 I have called Jubæa Speciosa, a splendid Palm. In the year 1855 I sent you some plants under the name of Palmist of Round Island I was since told by a Gentleman who called here a traveller & who appeared to know the plant that its name was Jubæa Spectabilis, said it was a very rare plant. He also told me that the plants I sent you under the name of Euterpe Carobœa was Oreodoxa Regia which appears to me to be correct as I have since received that plant from South America. No 8 I think belongs to the same family as the one from Round Island, only it is a much larger tree & altogether a more beautiful plant, I have therefor called it Jubæa Speciosa as I think it highly merits the name. It is not plentiful I was at one time afraid I should have been obliged to leave the Island without it as I could neither find seeds nor young plants of it. I offered money to the natives if they could bring me seeds but they could find none. After having finished my general survey of the Island I had two days to spare, I therefor started again with a determination to get the smalest plant I could find if I could get no seeds, in a small glen near the Sea I found three young plants one of them I now send you, and soon afterwards I found [a] dry seed raceme hanging on the tree with a few seeds still in it (I have sent you one of the seedlings). The Island abounds with rats, Guinea fowels & Pigs I expect some of them eat the seeds which makes the plants so scarce.

No 6 is an Areca & very plentiful the seeds ware not ripe at the time I was there I however brought home some of the ripest I could find and have reared some plants from them. This might truly be called the Cabbage Palm as the tender heart is realy very good, when I felt hungry I used to cut down a tree and eat a lunch of the tender part, and the other Gentlemen brought quantities of the tops to Mauritius with them for their friends.[3]

The letter continues in similar vein, ending with a reference to his latest contribution to the Kew Museum. 'I fancy seeds of these new palms would be interesting to your Museum I have therefor sent for that purpose a few dry seeds of all the four species of Latania you will know these by their seeds afterwards.' The seeds were listed in the Entry Book five months later, on 24th November, 1858, under the species names *L. rubia*, *L. glaucophylla*, *L. aurea*, and *L. Bourbonnais*.

Another Museum entry, in 1857, refers to '2 double cocoa nuts showing method of germination'. These might be the two *Lodoicea* seeds which in this same letter James said had been sent to Kew in 1857, but which John Smith later reported were rotten.

An eye witness account of the appearance of the Botanic Garden at this period is provided by the unpublished Journal of John Edward Moffat, a British Army Staff Surgeon. He was on his way to India, when he stopped off in Mauritius for a few days in October 1858.

> 20th Went with Stirling and Capt [—] to Pamplemousses, the latter provided with a letter of introduction to Mr Duncan the superintendant and manager of the government gardens at that place. After a very pretty drive of about 6 miles, through Malabar towns, and along a road lined the whole way with various shops and native tradesmen and crowded with natives, with sugar canes in all directions, we reached our destination, and luckily met Mr Duncan at the entrance, who most kindly conducted us all over the gardens and showed us every thing worth seeing, very luckily for us I say, for the trees being all foreign and tropical, were unknown to us. I was rather dissapointed expecting to see a flower garden, instead of which there was nothing but trees – these were interesting it's true, from the great no. of species of each there, and their variety and novelty, but one gets fatigued among 50 acres of Palms, Bamboos, etc., and flowers are my weakness. There were a few wild looking roses – However I was gratified by the sight of beautiful collections of wild ferns, which are abundant in the Island.[7]

Although interesting, this account is odd. How was it that Moffat did not see all the roses specifically mentioned by William Ellis when he visited the Garden five years earlier? It is possible that James was reducing the space devoted to flower borders, making the Garden into something more like the arboretum that we see today, but this seems unlikely given the number of roses listed in his *Catalogue of Plants* of 1863. Perhaps Moffat was exhausted by the trees and made his excuses before James had a chance of showing him the flower borders.

James certainly did not ignore plants other than trees, far from it. The following year, in September 1859, Mauritius was the location for what sounds like an international flower and livestock show.

We have just had an inter-colonial exhibition which has been a splendid affair, far exceeding the expectations of every one in Mauritius, Bourbon contributed largely and in fruits of the Citrus tribes they beat Mauritius hollow, their Vanilla was also splendid, Ceylon was second in Coffee — Mauritius Sugar was splendid none of the Colonies had any chance. In plants & flowers your humble servant carried all before him, Vegetables were very fine no one would have thought they had been grown under a tropical Sun, our Governors Collection got the first prize.

Animals were fine and in great variety including Elephants & Lions. Camels, Horses, Cows, and indeed allmost every living thing.

Lady's Work, Paintings, Photographs Etc were very fine, with the exception of Pine Apples Bourbon made the best fruits such as Oranges, Citrons, Shaddocks, Mandarines & Lemons — their Climate being cooler is better adapted for those things.

But to attempt to inumerate the things exhibited would take much more time than I can spare.[8]

James was showered with medals, issued by the Royal Society of Arts and Sciences of Mauritius: one each of 1st class gold (value £10), 2nd class gold (value £5), and 3rd class silver for a collection of 55 specimens of fibres; plus three bronze medals for pineapples and cut flowers.

The Exhibition was open for four days and the medals were distributed by his Excellency the Governor on the last day. The immense crowd assembled were delighted to find their Garden which was but a few years back considered a disgrace to them, so successful, and when the first class Medal was handed to me by the Governor for the general excellance of my contributions to the exhibition, the immense crowd assembled cheered me.

Our present Governor is a man who wishes to advance and promote Science in every way in his power as well as to advance the general interests of the colony he is certainly by far the best and ablest Governor I have seen in Mauritius, and well deserving of any honor that can be given him.

I would therefore beg to suggest that the large leafed Palm that I sent you from the Seychelle Islands should be named after him. I would allways consider that the native names should be taken into consideration, the native name of this fine Palm is the large leaved Latania but is certainly not a latania at all, its seeds are quite round. I therefor propose that it be called Stevensonia grandifolia as I was the first to bring it into notice I think I am intitled to have some voice in its name. I shall await your reply on this subject which you will please let me have at your earliest oppertunity.

15

GOOD NEWS – AND BAD NEWS

James's admiration of Sir William Stevenson, governor from 1857 until his death in 1863, seems to have been reciprocated. In 1858 the governor, who was a botanist himself, praised James's 'good practical and scientific knowledge'.[1] James had acquired this scientific knowledge from his practical experience, as a gardener and as a plant collector. However, there was inevitably a limit to what could be achieved in a nineteenth century colonial botanic garden. Few of them had much in the way of scientific resources, or were in a position to do taxonomic work – this was almost always carried out back in Britain. So what should be the future development of Pamplemousses? James promoted the idea that 'the usefulness of the Botanical Garden [lay in] the introduction, propagation, and distribution of plants.' This economic benefit was appreciated by the authorities in Port Louis, but it did depend on a regular two way flow of plant specimens. There was also the question of the conservation of endemic plants, and James was shortly to recommend the setting up of a museum or herbarium.

However, these things could not be done without more help, not least because James had now spent ten uninterrupted years in the tropics, and was beginning to feel exhausted. (By 1858 he was 56, which was unusually old for a tropical botanic garden director in the nineteenth century.)[2] He needed to make plans for the future. And there was also the question of money – both his salary and that of the other staff in the Botanic Garden.

In May 1858, James took the opportunity of a departmental review to send the colonial secretary an argument for a complete rethink of the manner in which the Garden was funded. The letter was carefully crafted. Not only is the handwriting clear, but the text is (almost) free from spelling 'errors'. Someone – perhaps Sarah or one of the boys? – must have gone over a draft before the final copy was written.

Sir

As I understand all the Departments are being revised in order to place each on an efficient footing

I therefore beg to annex for His Excellency the Governor's information, such an addition as I think necessary to render efficient the Establishment of the Botanical Garden

I have also named the Salaries, which I consider to be merely a fair remuneration for the services of men capable of filling such situations in this expensive Colony.

The following additions will appear to be a considerable increase, compared with the previous expenditure but it should be at the same time borne in mind, that the Garden was in 1849 when I took charge, almost a jungle or forest, without even being enclosed by a fence and the only labour then bestowed upon it, was sweeping up dead leaves, and keeping a portion of the walks free from weeds.

Very few young plants were at that time propagated for distribution, or exportation & but very few new ones were introduced into the Colony. Much has of late been done by Prison Labour towards fencing in and improving a portion of the Garden, but a very great deal still remains to be done; That portion of the Garden which has been cleared and trenched has been replanted with newly introduced plants.

From Fifteen to Twenty Thousand young plants are now annually propagated and distributed to the inhabitants of the Colony, and often I have large demands for plants which I am unable to comply with owing to the limited assistance allowed to the Establishment.

In most countries, Botanical Gardens are only expected to give a few cuttings or plants to Nurserymen, who make a living by propagating them for sale, but there being no Nurserymen in this Colony, the Botanical Garden is the only place where plants can be obtained. It may therefore be considered not only a Botanical Garden, but also a Nursery for the whole Island.

With regard to the introduction of new plants, I may remark that there is scarcely a Botanical Establishment of any note in the World, that I am not in correspondence with, and that scarcely a month passes but I receive in, and send away Cases of plants by exchange.

This very large increase in correspondence and Propagation of plants etc etc renders an Assistant Director indispensable, as the work cannot be properly got through without such assistance.

In making those additions & alterations the usefulness of the Botanical Garden for the introduction, propagation, and distribution of plants, bearing in mind that it is the only place where they can be had in Mauritius, should be brought into consideration.

If a rich and prosperous Colony can obtain all these advantages and enjoyments for its Inhabitants, at the small annual cost of £1384 (the annual expences of a small Nursery in England considerably exceeds this amount) surely it must be admitted that they are to be had on very reasonable terms.

It is I beleive the wish of the Public at large that this establishment should be put on an efficient footing, – both on account of its utility, and also on account of its being the only place where they can enjoy the healthful pleasure of a Garden.

I must however mention that the increase now asked for is in addition to the band of 20 Prisoners at present allowed. They were only intended for very heavy works, such as Fencing in the Garden, deepening Canals, Trenching ground, removing stones & large roots of Trees etc etc. When all such works are finished, they will then be no longer required in the Botanical Garden.

On your perusing these remarks, I flatter myself, Sir, that you will be at once convinced of the reasonableness of all my demands. I therefore hope to be favoured with the aid of your influence towards putting this very useful Establishment on an efficient and permanent footing.

I have the honor to be etc.

	Annual Salary [£]
Director	400
Allowance for petty expenses	100
Asst. Director	200
Overseer of Workmen	72
Carpenter	48
Gatekeeper	36
10 Laborers at £1.12.0 each per month	192
20 do. at £1.8.0 each per month	<u>336</u>
	<u>1384</u>

The letter was referred the next day to the auditor, and two days after that (what speed!) there was a formal response, signed by both the auditor general and the treasurer:

> We have reason to believe that the Statement made by Mr Duncan is correct, and that the Botanical Garden has arrived at its present comparatively satisfactory state thro' his unremitting diligence, and we bear willing testimony to the prompt attention which he has on every occasion given to the numerous requisitions made on him for seeds and plants.
>
> There can be no doubt as to the value of this Garden in a scientific point of view and to the advantages of constant communication and exchange with other Establishments of a similar nature in every part of the world.
>
> The application of the Director appears to us reasonable and justified by the circumstances of the case, and we have the honor to submit it for favorable consideration.
>
> The salaries attached to this Establishment are already provided for in Appendix E of the Scale recommended by the Committee with the exception of that of the Assistant Director, a new appointment for which we beg to recommend a salary of £200 per annum, on the Scale allotted to the 3rd Class of Government Officers.
>
> 28th May 1858[3]

So far so good. But the wheels of government can turn slowly. Such radical changes needed to be approved by the Colonial Office in London, to which the governor wrote on 14th October. He also set up a Special Committee to examine the Garden. This reported on 20th September that an assistant to the director was indeed much needed and that one should be appointed on a temporary basis pending a reply from the secretary of state. A person named Skelhorne was appointed, but he did not last long, being 'unequal to the duties'. James expressed the hope that Sir William Hooker could suggest someone suitable.

Nothing much had happened for about a year, when, in November 1859, a document appeared that listed James in a class of public servants whose salaries would start at £300 – which, as he pointed out at once, would be no increase over what he was already getting.

> I may mention that I have had charge of the Botanical Gardens for upwards of Ten Years, a period sufficiently long to merit some reward, especially as, during that time the Gardens have, through my labour and exertions, not only been highly useful to this Colony but also to Botanical Science throughout the world. This has, on several occasions, been acknowledged by Sir W J Hooker, the Director of the Royal Botanical Gardens at Kew, and in the last Report on Kew Gardens, this Establishment is specially mentioned as one of the principal contributors of new Plants to that Establishment.
>
> After having toiled so long and so arduously to obtain this satisfactory result, I feel confident that Your Excellency will sympathise with my feelings of disappointment on finding myself placed on so low a class.[4]

This letter was forwarded to the Civil Service Commissioners on Public Establishments, who confirmed the need for an upgrading: 'We are of opinion that much, which cannot be performed with the present staff, is wanting to make the Garden of the importance & utility it should be.'[5] For good measure, the commissioners confirmed the need for a complete catalogue of plants in the Garden. Such a catalogue was already in preparation but could not be finished for a long time unless through the appointment of an assistant director.

These arguments eventually produced results. On 22nd September 1860, James received an official letter from the colonial secretary's office, cool but civil, informing him that he was to be put on a salary scale rising from £400 to £600 with effect from 1st July 1859.[6] One can imagine the celebrations that took place in the Botanic Garden director's house that evening, not least because just a fortnight before, James and Sarah had acquired a new grandchild. He was named George, after his late uncle, and was born to Frances Maria on 8th September.

The government letter went on to say that so far as the assistant was concerned, James should as soon as possible provide a job description which would be forwarded to the secretary of state in London for onward transmission to Sir William Hooker. The assistant director's salary would start at £150 or £200 depending on the qualifications of the person selected.

The very same day, James wrote out a list of services to be provided and qualifications required:

1.— To assist in Corespondence & in recording the same.
2.— Propagating choice plants.
3.— Potting & packing Plants for Exportation.
4.— Making collections of seeds in the Garden — as well as in the Forests of the Island, & naming the same.
5.— Collecting and naming Specimens of Plants, for forming Herbariums.
6.— Collecting Specimens of Timbers, Fibres etc etc for Museums.
7.— Distributing Plants to the Public when applied for.
8.— Many newly introduced & delicate plants would require his constant care.
9.— To assist in the general Superintendance of the Garden.

In order that he should be able to perform the above mentioned services satisfactorily, I submit that he should be Possesed of the following Qualifications.
viz

1.— He should have a considerable knowledge of Botany, & be able to conduct corespondence on that subject.
2.— He should have a good practical knowledge of the Cultivation & Propagation of Plants Generally.—
3.— He should be a Sober, Steady & Industrious Man, & I think it would be desirable that he should be a married man.[7]

It would appear that James was writing out here a job description for a director of the Botanic Garden, perhaps anticipating his own departure, rather than that of an assistant. However, all the documents were packaged up and sent off to the Duke of Newcastle, the new secretary of state, on 19th October 1860. James was jubilant. In a letter he wrote to Sir William Hooker, he was quite skittish and got tied up in a complicated metaphor in which Governor Stevenson became the captain of a ship.

Sir William

I duly received your letter and was very glad to hear your health had so much improved, & felt much obliged for your kind inquiries after my health. Some days I feel pretty well, but never for long together, 12 years hard toiling under a Tropical Sun has given me a sad shaking, of late I have been obliged to take great care of myself, I am anxiously looking forward to getting leave of absence to see if the climate of dear old England will brace me up again — I have become so attached to the Garden here and all my pot plants, that I could not bear the thought of leaving them uncared, and unprovided for — I was therefor anxious to get an efficient assistant appointed to take charge before I left them — To accomplish this has been a long fatiguing job. I for a long time past thought I had a good friend in the Captain at the helm, and beleived he would take charge of the vessel if I could only pilate her into port — but as she had to pass through many dangers before he could have full charge of her, I of course felt very anxious about her safety. <u>She is now safe in port & the Captain promised her good.</u>

During the time you was unwell I hade several times written to Mr. Smith, telling him from time to time how anxious I was to get an assistant, and also about carrying out various other improvements. I sometimes thought he doubted if I should ever succeed, I have therefore sent copies of the concluding papers under cover to him, in order that he might see that I had succeeded, when he has read them I have told him to hand them over to you, as you will no doubt soon hear officially from the Government about the Assistant, & I wish you to clearly understand the case.

All the salaries here are now placed upon a sort of sliding scale advancing by annual increments to a certain amount.

You will see that my Assistant is to have £150, rising to £250 — or £200 rising to £300 according to the description of man that may be selected. Now this will be in a great measure left for you to decide — It appears to me that you should view the case this way — This man is going as an assistant to service a kind of apprenticeship, preparatory to becoming Director, when he has learned the language and become capable. It is therefore necessary that he should be a clever man, a good Botanist & so forth, and if so the higher amount of salary will be none too much for him at present. One thing is omitted in the Governor's letter, <u>a house</u>, ...

I think the man you select should be a <u>married man</u> a single man coming out to this Colony would be likely to make a very bad choice of a wife if he married, but if he did not, he would most likely do worse.

I would also like him to be a Protestant. I do not know if the Government will pay his passage out, or not, but I think they ought to do so — but if not I think the P & O Company carries Government servants at a reduced scale — a Second Class passage by their vessels would I think be preferable to a cabin passage on board of a sailing ship to say <u>nothing about the time</u>, as on board these steamers there is plenty of good provisions, medical attendance, etc etc, & these things at sea are of very great importance to health & comfort.

I had allmost forgotten to mention another reason for giving my assistant the higher rate of salary, that is, that the sugar planters are allways anxious to obtain intelligent men as managers on their Estates for the first few years they would not take him, as he would be perfectly unacquainted with the language generally spoken here and consequently unfit to carry on any establishment but in a few years time the case would be different, he would then be much more usefull and they would then be very glad to get him, but if you give him the higher rate of salary I think he would not be likely to leave the Garden. . . .

I trust Sir William you are now in the enjoyment of good health & that I will have the pleasure of hearing from you again. Believe me Sir William
Yours very Respectfully[8]

Having, as he thought, fixed up the appointment of his successor, and despatched the letter to Hooker, James next addressed to the colonial secretary a memorandum with suggestions for improvements to the Garden itself.

He proposed the setting up of a museum of dried specimens of plants, timbers, fibres, and seeds. 'Botanical Gardens can hardly be considered as complete without a small Museum containing such a collection.' The main expense would be a suitable building. Because wood encouraged insects, he suggested that an iron building should be ordered from Britain. 'It might be ornamental and light in appearance . . . A wide verandah round it would also form an excellent shelter for visitors during heavy showers of rain.' The Garden also needed a suitable lodge-gate at the entrance for the use of the guardian, and accommodation for the new assistant director.[9]

The memorandum is accompanied in the file by several comments in other hands, including one proposing a design for the assistant director's house. It would be a simple structure measuring 36 feet by 16 feet, with a broad verandah all the way round. A central parlour would have a bedroom on one side, and a dining room on the other.[10]

Everything at last seemed to be going James's way. But then, in the New Year, it all went sour. On 28th February 1861 he was sent a perfectly reasonable letter from the colonial secretary's office, to the effect that the secretary of state in London had now approved the post of assistant director, but that Sir William Hooker at Kew was not able to 'procure the services of a Gentleman possessing all the high qualifications mentioned in your letter of the 22nd September last'. There would, however, be no difficulty in finding 'a very superior man as Head

Gardener, possessing some, but not much, ordinary botanical knowledge'. James was reminded that the scientific duties proposed by him should be performed by himself. The assistant had been recommended in order to carry out routine work, leaving James free to devote more time to 'subjects of higher importance'. Would he confirm that the recruitment could proceed along those lines?[11]

James, however, had not received this letter when he wrote, also on 28th February, to John Smith, the curator at Kew, in response to a letter which has not survived. Carefully written on four pages of lightweight pale blue paper, the letter mixes botany with personal and professional anguish in a strange way.

28th February 1861

My dear Sir

I herewith send you a few more dried Specimens of Ferns, and must at the sametime beg to remind you, that you have taken no notice of the last lot I sent you. These now sent are not in very good condition, and that is not to be wondered at considering that they lay soaked in water for seven days during the late Hurricane here.— I am by no means certain that all the Adiantum are distinct Species as sometimes I have fancied that several of them were the same, and at other times I have fancied they were different, so I thought I had better send them to you for examination.— The three specimens of A. asarifolium are sent for your herbarium, I have long intended paying a visit to the locality where it grows, but as it was a long distance from here one thing or another has allways prevented my doing so, lately my eldest son who is a land surveyor was going near that quarter, and I asked him to look and see if he could find any plants of it, fortunately he found a fine patch and brought them home with him, and these leaves are therefore from its native locality — The plants I have potted and I hope to be able to save them, and also to send you one by & bye when they get established in their new abode.

I duly received your letter per the preavious mail and the other day I received one from Sir W.J.Hooker informing one that he could not assist us in recommending a suitable man for the Situation of Assistant Director, in our Garden — Now my dear Sir I never for a moment calculated upon receiving such an answer from Sir William I had all along from the first kept you fully informed of what was going on here, you were therefore aware of the many difficulties I had to contend with both here and in England, and that the first Salary settled upon was only one hundred pounds per Annum (certainly much too low for Mauritius). I could only get over this settlement by strongly repeating to the Authorities, that, a suitable man could not be got for that sum, and when I was called upon to state the qualifications required for an Assistant Director, I was obliged to put them high in order to get a suitable salary decided uppon, up to the very last you will see that they were undecided about the Salary, and that it was only after I had sent in those qualifications that they agreed to place him on the scale I had recommended viz £200 rising by annual increments of £10 to £300 with regard to this scale of increments you must not suppose that they are paid as a matter of course as the rule is that they are only allowed every year after a certificate to the following effect has been sent to the Governor from the Chief of the Department, viz That the party has been sober and industrious and conducted himself to his Chief's satisfaction during the year. After this certificate has been sent in, and approved the payment of the increment is authorized by the Governor, without that certificate it cannot be paid. The house question would have been at once put to rights by Sir William representing its necessity.

The Answer I expected from Kew or that Sir William might have given was something like the following — That a man possessing all the qualifications required, could not be got for the salary named, but that if a House was also allowed, Sir W.J. Hooker could recommend a man possessing all the qualifications that he considered was necessary for the subordinate situation of Assistant Director of the Botanical Gardens at Mauritius.— an answer such as the above might have caused a little delay, if the Duke of Newcastle had considered it necessary to have referred the case back here, but I do not think he would have done so, but at worst it would have left the affair open, and it would soon have been put right again — whereas the answer Sir W. has given, if like what he has sent to me places the affair in a very critical position, indeed, if I understand it rightly he has in fact closed the affair so far at least as your Establishment is concerned, by stating that he cannot assist us in recommending a suitable man.— So far I have heard nothing from the Government here, perhaps the Home Government may not have forwarded Sir William's answer yet, as soon as I hear something about the affair I will answer his Sir William's letter, in the mean time you can tell Sir William what I have said here and how dissappointed I feel — of course you are not exempt yourself as I find you were one of the parties consulted on the Subject. – In your last letter you stated that you had a man in your eye that you thought would suit me if nothing more can be done through your establishment I think it would be a good plan to get him to apply for the situation, at the same time producing the best testimonials he can get from influential parties — As to the Passage for the Wife I do not think that would be allowed as I have never known an instance of the kind, a sum however would be allowed for his own passage — when I came here I was obliged to pay my own passage, my salary was £250 per annum and all I could get was half salary during the time I was at Sea — As to the House I have no doubt but that will be put to rights as soon as the affair is brought on again. — I have sent you a newspaper by the presant mail, you will thereby see some accounts of the terrable Hurricane we have had here, it lasted nearly a week, our Garden is in an Awful State, as yet we hardly know the extent of the dammage done, but there is no doubt many choice plants have been destroyed, & Trees by hundreds, many lives have been lost, and cattle drowned out of number, many houses are unroofed & blown down.

You will also see the Sad Loss we have had in our family by the Melancholy Death of my eldest Grand-Child, poor little dear she strayed out at the door unseen and was drowned close to the house. She was a fine intelligant Child two years & three months old, her sad death was a terrable shock to us.— The celebrated Pampas Grass is in flower here at presant, the flower resembles that of the sugar cane only not half so fine, it will be thought nothing of here.

Believe me My dear Sir

Yours very truly

James Duncan

The shifts in tone in the letter seem to a modern reader rather shocking, but they could be a characteristic of James's personality, or perhaps how personal tragedy was sometimes handled in the nineteenth century.[12]

To add to the family's grief over Charlotte Sarah, news must soon have arrived of the death of James's father in Aberdeen. A few months earlier, James had written to a friend, John Ferguson, asking him to visit his father in order to find out how he was. Ferguson wrote back on 14th December, so the letter would have reached Mauritius just about the time of the great storm.

Ferguson's letter had brought not very cheerful news. James's father was 'exceedingly frail' and had made a bad speculation in property, losing £1000. The sum of £150, which James had at some point sent home to his father, had been swallowed up in interest and legal expenses, but William was anxious to have this bond discharged before he died. He was planning to leave his entire estate to James's half sister Helen Jane – 'thinking as he says that you are not in want of anything from him. . . . I don't think your sister means to impose upon you — she seems to me a very easy sort of person who does not understand money matters very much.' This is the first record we have of James's financial position, to which we will return.[13]

William Duncan died on 6th January and was buried in the depths of a northern winter in the same Aberdeen cemetery as his brother John, and alongside his wife Margaret, James's stepmother. The gravestone, which had originally been erected by William for Margaret, in due course recorded the deaths of no fewer than four other members of the family, their names and relationships carved in handsome lettering in the soft sandstone. This stone is, however, much more vulnerable to wind and weather than the harder granite more commonly used in Aberdeen, and while (ironically) James's granite memorial stands virtually indestructible in its limestone Wiltshire graveyard, his father's memorial, surrounded though it is by stones of grey granite, is rapidly returning to its elements.

Through the first half of 1861, the correspondence about an assistant director for the Garden meandered on, involving (in addition to James) the colonial secretary in Port Louis, the governor, the Duke of Newcastle, and Sir William Hooker. Sir William was still involved in Mauritian affairs, but he was now 75, and had handed over many of his responsibilities to his son Joseph, who had become his deputy at Kew in 1855.[14] There was a to-ing and a fro-ing over numerous details: the rental value of the assistant director's house, whether or not the government would provide an allowance for bringing out the successful candidate's wife, when and how salary increments would be given, and so on. Eventually, at the end of June, an appointment was made, and Sir William Hooker was thanked by the Duke of Newcastle's assistant for the trouble he had taken 'about the Mauritian Gardener'.[15]

On 4th January the following year (1862), James could report that 'Mr & Mrs Horne arrived here on the 30th of last month having made the passage in 81 days, they are both in good health.'[16] With them came a case of plants, mostly azaleas, though unfortunately only two of them survived the journey. However, John Horne himself turned out to be an inspired choice.

16

CATALOGUE OF PLANTS

I have found almost no letters written by James Duncan from the year 1862. Presumably he felt that he had achieved his aims with regard to the colonial government in Port Louis, while the arrival of John Horne meant that he at last had someone with whom he could discuss matters gardening and botanical, relieving him of the need to lay out his excitements and worries in epistles to Sir William Hooker. John Horne had been a trainee gardener at Kew and would have been able to tell James much about what had been happening there in the past decade. Intelligent and able, although he did not become full director at Pamplemousses until 1876, he was appointed acting director on James's retirement.

The main task on which James was now engaged was the compilation of the *Catalogue of Plants in the Royal Botanical Garden*, Mauritius, which was published in Port Louis in 1863. Compilation of such a work had been under intermittent discussion ever since James's early days on the island. In September 1860 he had written to the colonial secretary in answer to an enquiry as to what published information regarding plants growing in Mauritius was currently available. He explained that the only catalogue was *Hortus Mauritianus* published by the late Professor Bojer in 1837, but now out of print. A Dr Ayers was collecting material for a catalogue of indigenous plants, while Louis Bouton had published in 1857 a small work on medicinal plants.[1]

Bojer's catalogue listed 2,000 species, and attempted to differentiate between native and exotic species. This had been preceded by a catalogue of the exotic plants growing in Mauritius, written by Dr J.V. Thompson and published in 1816. An 1822 revision included some indigenous plants, but both works were long out of print.[2]

The subject of a new reference book of Mauritian plants also came up in correspondence with Sir William Hooker. James wrote in June 1861:

You mention that you are in correspondence with the Duke of Newcastle respecting a good Flora of Mauritius, and which you have fully answered & somewhat in connection with an assistant to the Garden. As you have not mentioned in what way you would recommend the conection with the Garden I cannot of course give any opinion but I can scarcely see in what way they could be advantageously connected.— "You then say nothing is done here as in Mr Bojer's time." Mr Bojer was Professor of Botany in the Royal College at Port Louis and Curator of the Museum of Natural History at the same place, we have had no Professor of Botany since his death, but I hear two new Professors have just come by the Mail from Edinburgh, as they are both for the Scientific Classes I think it is probable one of them will be to replace Mr Bojer, as I hear their salary is £500 per annum or upwards each. . . .

Dr Ayres is collecting materials for Publishing a Flora of the Island, and I have been giving him everything that came in my way to assist him, but the duties required of me at the Garden is far more than I can attend to, consequently I have but little time to spare, and Dr Ayres has a great deal on his hands also. There can be no doubt but that a clever Botanist who could devote some time to the subject is much wanted in Mauritius.[3]

It would seem that Kew wanted a Flora of Mauritius, rather than merely a Catalogue, but in general, they preferred these to be written by their own man rather than an enthusiast on the ground who did not 'belong' to Kew. This was a conflict that was to arise in Australia with respect to Ferdinand von Mueller. *The major Flora of Mauritius and the Seychelles* by Kew's J.G. Baker was eventually to be published in 1877, but this work undoubtedly suffered from the fact that the author never visited the islands, relying entirely on correspondence and herbarium specimens.[4] Meanwhile, there was a gap to be filled, and with local encouragement from Port Louis, James accomplished this. It is perhaps significant that James got on so well with Sir William Stevenson, though the governor died of dysentery in January 1863, and so never saw the completed work. His successor, however, Sir Henry Barkly, was a distinguished botanist in his own right. His previous posting was in Victoria and he encouraged plant exchanges between Pamplemousses and Melbourne.

There was a precedent for the Mauritian work in the *Catalogue of the Plants under Cultivation in the Government Botanic Garden, Adelaide, South Australia*. This had been published in 1859 and listed 2880 species, about the same number as James's Catalogue, and was, like that, organised in alphabetical order by genus. Local names were given for genera, but not for species.

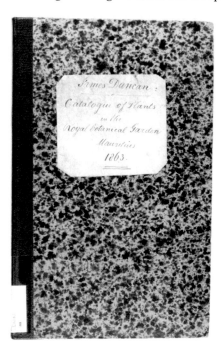

The *Catalogue of Plants in the Royal Botanical Garden Mauritius* is a quarto volume of 104 pages, printed on pale blue paper and published by H. Plaideau, Government Printer.[5] James laid out his aims in the Preface, dated 23rd February 1863, the full text of which runs as follows:

To compile a Catalogue of the Plants cultivated in a Botanical Garden, where no work of the kind previously existed, is attended with a considerable amount of labour and difficulty. I must, therefore, notwithstanding the great care and trouble I have taken to make this work as complete and correct as possible, beg the indulgence of the Authorities, as well as that of the Public, should it be found that any errors or omissions have unavoidably crept into it. In a Colony so subject to hurricanes as Mauritius is, the number of plants under cultivation will often vary, in proof of which I need only refer to the last severe hurricane in February 1861, which lasted a whole week,— (an unusua[l] length of time).— During that week, a large number of valuable Plants perished, some of which we have not as yet been able to reintroduce. This Catalogue will, however, render the getting up of future editions a work of much less labour, as they will be to a considerable extent the same. It is hoped it will be useful to the Public of Mauritius, and also to Correspondents in other Countries, by affording them the means of readily ascertaining what our Collection consists of, and thereby giving such information, as is required to secure an advantageous system of exchange of Plants to both parties. I may mention that we are most desirous of introducing such Plants as are interesting for their utility, or their beauty, and that any information respecting their uses, or peculiarity in their mode of cultivation will, at all times, be very acceptable. This Catalogue is arranged alphabetically, which I consider the most suitable system for a Garden Catalogue, as it affords the most ready means of reference. The natural orders are given, according to the arrangement of the Vegetable Kingdom by Doctor Lindley, and also the authorities as far as possible for both genera and species. An Index of abbreviations, and another of local names, is also given. The latter, it is hoped, will be useful to the Inhabitants of the Island.

I have marked with an a in a parenthesis, thus (a), the exotic Plants that have been introduced since I took charge of the Garden, and also such native Plants that I have introduced from the Forests and brought under cultivation; the latter will easily be known from the former, the native countries being given. This will at once give some idea of the extent to which the Garden, and thereby the Island, has been enriched by the introduction or cultivation of both native and exotic plants. We have also a number of plants, the names of which are as yet unknown; they have been received from the interior of Africa, Madagascar, &c., &c., without names, and have not as yet flowered here; many of them have probably never been described by any Botanist.

It has been very gratifying to me to witness, year after year, the extending love of plants, as well as Horticulture in general, amongst the inhabitants of this Colony, which must always afford a healthy and instructive recreation, and add greatly to the beauty of their premises, and to the Colony at large. I have also had great pleasure in always trying to meet the increasing demands for Plants; and to show to what extent I have done so, I need only mention that, during the past year, twenty-five thousand nine hundred and twenty-five (25,925) Plants have been distributed from the Garden to the inhabitants of the Colony.

When the immense labour of propagation that is expended to enable me to deliver over to the public such a large number of Plants in one year, as that above mentioned, the time taken up in accompanying visitors round the Garden, in receiving imported cases of Plants, and refilling them for exportation, together with the extensive correspondence which such transactions give rise to, is considered, as well as the numerous other duties connected with the Gardens, I trust that no apology, on my part will be deemed necessary for the delay which has taken place in bringing this work before the Public.

JAMES DUNCAN.

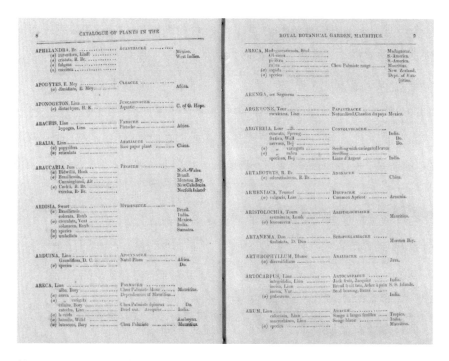

About 2400 species of plants are listed in the catalogue, more than half of which are marked with an '(a)' to indicate that they had been introduced to Pamplemousses during James's time as director. Rouillard notes that among the large number of plants introduced are more than a hundred palm species, including the following: *Acromia sclerocarpa*, and *A. totai*, *Aiphanes caryotifolia* and *A. elegans*, *Livistona rotundifolia* and *L. saribus*, *Thrinax excelsa* and *T. radiata*, *Arenga pinnata*, *Attalea cohune*, *Licuala spinosa*, *Sabal palmetto* and above all the majestic royal palm, *Roystonea regia*, successors of which still line Poivre Avenue today.[6] James also introduced a large number of ferns (perhaps showing the influence of Sir William Hooker, since ferns were Hooker's best-known academic interest), orchids, begonias, gloxinias, and 167 varieties of rose. Among the ornamental plants were many species of azalea, camelia, gardenia, and jasmine, and acanthuses with multicoloured leaves. One of the roses listed in the catalogue is 'Rosa Indica Noisettiana Caroline Duncan', named after James's daughter.

James Duncan's introduction of bougainvillea caused a sensation which must have been similar to the effect in Britain of Kew's introduction of rhododendrons ten years earlier, when 'a kind of gasp of amazement ran through the whole gardening world.'[7] In Mauritius, a newspaper correspondent, Charles Baissac, claimed in June 1862 that 'aujourd'hui il faut être un haut fonctionnaire du gouvernement pour viser à devenir propriétaire d'un *Bougainvillea splendens.*[8]

Not everyone was pleased. Baissac regretted that the axe had been put to hundred year old trees planted by Poivre and Céré. 'Nous avons compris que le règne des canneliers est passé et que les manguiers du jardin étaient détronnés par les espèces introduites postérieurement.'[9] It is true that the Garden no longer showed its origin as a spice plantation. But Baissac drew attention also to the beautiful lake recently created, with small islands looking like floating groves. This was the 'Grand Bassin' which previously had had uncertain and muddy banks.

The Garden had other important additions at this time. A white marble obelisk was erected in 1861 at a crossing on Labourdonnais Avenue. It was a gift to the Royal Society of Arts and Sciences of Mauritius from François Liénard de Lamivoye. Born in 1782, he had arrived in Mauritius as a child and had led an adventurous life: he had fought against the British, had been captured more than once, and had been imprisoned in India. He was now an enthusiastic member of the Royal Society of Arts and Sciences, of which he was one of the founders.

The four sides of the Liénard obelisk are engraved with the names of the principal benefactors of the island: those who contributed to the prosperity of the island through agriculture, and enriched it by the introduction of plants and animals of interest. On the base is engraved a quotation from Bernardin de Saint-Pierre: 'Le don d'une plante utile me paraît plus précieux que le découverte d'une mine d'or et un monument plus durable qu'une pyramide.'[10]

Another Botanic Garden project was the installation of the elaborate iron gates which still stand today at the entrance to the Garden. In 1861, James informed the governor that an iron gate and grill had arrived from Britain but that he was not yet in a position to erect them. It would seem that the gates were then taken to Port Louis, where they were erected outside the Supreme Court, only returning to Pamplemousses to be put up in their final position in 1868. It is said that they had received first prize in an international exhibition held at Crystal Palace in London. The gates and their surrounds cost a total of £2198.[11]

17

DEPARTURE

Meanwhile, the exchange of plants with Kew continued. Although no letter from Sir William Hooker to James Duncan seems to have survived, there does exist one from Sir William's son, Joseph, who wrote to Mauritius from Kew on 4th August 1863.

My dear Sir

I have the pleasure of sending you from Sir W. Hooker, a case of living plants, as per list enclosed, in care of Mr Power a young medical gentleman who goes out, with troops I believe, in the Isabella Blyth & who has kindly offered to keep an eye to the case. Mr Smith has sent instructions to Mr Power & will probably also write to you by this opportunity.

Since the despatch of this box we have received two cases from you in excellent condition, containing various very acceptable plants. Amongst them are some capital specimens of Tree Ferns, & of an Acrostichum (Platycerium) that is new to us. Also two noble Lycopodiums both in beautiful condition and some remarkably fine Dracaenas one with a small mottled leaf appears nearly allied to one we have received from West tropical Africa, from Mr Mann. Altogether the cases arrived in excellent condition.

We shall always be glad to receive from you lists of the <u>sorts</u> of plants you want, as well as the names of special desiderata to your collection. Have you for instance many American Aroids, Cacti etc etc or do you want Australian things many of which, as the Queensland ones especially would I should think thrive in the Mauritius.

We are extremely anxious to get good collections of dried plants from Rodrigues & the Seychelle Islands, are such procurable?

I am very truly

Jos. D Hooker[1]

James replied on 5th October.

I was glad to hear that the two cases of Plants I sent per "Himalaya" had reached you in good condition, and so much to your satisfaction.

The case you sent me per "Isabella Blyth" had araived here before your letter, I therefore knew nothing of its coming untill I received the enclosed letter from Mr Power, the plants were not in very good condition and many of them dead.

You will see by Mr Power's letter that the case was full of fungus and that he opened it at sea and took out the dead plants, so far he done well, but unfortunately he watered the plants and by that means increased the evil however about twenty of them are alive and I hope will recover. The following are the numbers attached to the dead ones and which would have been new to us – 1 – 4 – 5 – 8 – 10 – 21 – 24 – 25 – 28 – 33 – 34. Several more were dead but we had allready got them and therefore they were of no importance.

As regards your question about Aroids & Cacti, we have a good many aroids here, and as to Cacti we could not grow them without protection as they rot during our hurricanes. After our Garden has been put into order, then we will be able to devote more time to such things, we might then be able to grow a collection of them under cover.

From Australia we receive a number of plants, we have Barklya syringafolia growing well here, and many other plants from that quarter.

Plants from South America and the West Indies, Western & Southern Africa suit us well, Bugainvilas are splendid here, by the way I have been rasing numbers of them from seed in order to get some new colours, one seedling has flowered this year of a splendid rich Magenta colour, B. speciosa & B. Glabra look quite poor beside it. I have about 100 seedlings got to flower.

I had written to Mr Smith asking him to send me a casefull of Cinchona plants as I think they would do well here but he has not sent them, after you receive this the season will be getting late but if the Autumn was mild they might still be sent, after they left the English Channel they would soon be in a warmer climate. If the season is suitable I would feel obliged by your sending them as soon as possible. —

Fifteen years hard work here has rendered a change of climate for a time at least necessary for both myself and my wife. We therefore think of visiting England next spring, most probably we will leave here by the March Mail.

If there is any plant here that you particularly want at Kew, if you will let me know I will endeavour to bring it home with me. My wife is at presant very poorly. Should her illness unfortunately continue long I may be obliged to leave here sooner but if it can be managed I will remain till March.

Please to make my kind respects to Sir W Hooker, I hope he is quite well.[2]

This is the first mention of an early departure from Mauritius, but things now moved quickly. James formally applied to the colonial secretary for leave of absence on 4th February 1864, and this was granted on the 24th: he was to have one year's leave on the understanding that he would stop off at Seychelles 'en passant'. The government would pay one-third of the cost of his passage.[3] A memo from the inspector general instructed a Sergeant Major Warren to 'give every assistance to Mr Duncan in carrying out his Botanical researches at the Seychelles and if possible provide him with a constable to accompany him & assist him in making his collection of plants'. The assistance included the provision of a boat.[4]

The stop over of a month was intended to result in the collection of plants and specimens for the proposed Flora of Mauritius and the Seychelles, to be written at Kew. Sir William himself had recently stated in a circular on Colonial Floras that nothing whatever was known about the Seychelles flora. Louis Bouton, curator of the Museum in Port Louis, wrote on 29th February to ask James if as many flowering plants as possible could be collected, pressed between two sheets of paper, and sent back to Mauritius with vernacular names and a note of where found. To help with the work, James asked if he could take with him one of his Indian labourers, named Ranjiah. 'He accompanied me on a similar excursion to the Island of Rodrigues and I found him very useful.'[5]

So James and Ranjiah, and presumably Sarah, though there is no mention of her, embarked on 6th March 1864 on the mail steamer, the Norma. But the stop over in Seychelles was aborted. James scribbled a note to the colonial secretary from on board the boat:

Sir,

I have only a moment to say that they would not allow me to land at the Seychelles, unless I would go into quarantine they would not even say when I could be taken out. I therefore declined going under those circumstances, and will proceed on to England. My man Ranjiah will be put into quarantine and sent back to Mauritius when he is released. Please to communicate all this to his Excellency the Governor, and I would be glad if you could let one of my sons know also.

In great haste, etc. etc.[6]

The civil commissioner in Seychelles who, to be fair, had only just been informed officially about James's impending arrival, wrote a reproachful letter to Port Louis in turn.

I regret to have to report that Mr Duncan did not land here on the arrival of the 'Norma' from Mauritius. The mail steamer always anchors at a distance of three miles from the shore. I did not go out to her, and the Captain could not wait until the question of giving immediate pratique to Mr Duncan could be referred to me. Mr Duncan declined to go to the station of observation pending the arrival of my reply, although this arrangement could only have involved a delay of one or two hours, but went on to Suez in the steamer.

I have directed Mr Duncan's servant, who landed here, to collect all the plants with which he was unacquainted, and they will be transmitted by the mail now due to His Excellency the Governor.[7]

While all this was going on, Governor Barkly wrote a long and carefully composed letter to the Duke of Newcastle at the Colonial Office in London, informing him that James Duncan had been granted leave of absence for one year and detailing the arrangements, including a grant to him of up to £20 to be spent by him on rare plants for Pamplemousses while he was in Britain. He went on to say that James had in fact asked for a break of a longer period than a year but that it would not be possible to leave the head gardener in charge for more than twelve months. In any case, the real reason for James's departure was the state of his health.

It would be far better for him to receive a retiring allowance, so as to make room for the appointment of some skilful Botanist under whose superintendance the materials for the publication of a Flora of the Mauritius and its Dependencies as contemplated by Sir William Hooker might be completed and properly arranged.

Some idea of this sort, Mr Duncan tells me, was entertained by the late Governor and it could be carried out at a very moderate cost.

I infer from my conversation with him that he would not object to resign at once if the Lords of the Treasury were disposed to sanction a liberal interpretation of the regulations in regard to his revenue so as to assign him about £200 per annum, and certainly after 15 years of what he truly terms laborious service in a tropical climate and when long past the sixtieth year of his age he would seem fully entitled to such a retiring allowance as will enable him to spend the rest of his days in ease and comfort.

His claims moreover are somewhat peculiar. He was sent out by the Secretary of State as Director of the Botanical Gardens at a time when they were little better than a wilderness, to return them to order, as well as to promote the introduction of a taste for the cultivation of Flowers, Fruit and Vegetables among the community at large.

How well he has succeeded in the first part of his work may be judged from the accompanying Catalogue of the Plants now to be found in the Gardens, a work which it must have cost him much trouble to compile as he has never made any pretensions to acquaintance with Scientific Botany. Towards the second object great progress has undoubtedly been made since his arrival here, and I believe he has always zealously co-operated in the efforts that have been made to get up shows etc. etc.

I trust therefore that his claim will meet with favourable consideration.[8]

It was only a year later that there was formal agreement from the Colonial Office that James should retire, so he remained nominally director of the Botanic Garden until March 1865. Now living at Rose Cottage, Harrow Weald,

Stanmore, in Middlesex, James wrote to the Colonial Office in February to ask that his position be settled. In order to calculate an appropriate pension, the Colonial Office decided to take advice from Sir William Hooker on how they should value the service provided by James Duncan during his years in Mauritius. He replied the following day – a remarkable achievement in someone who was now aged seventy-nine and who was in the last year of his life.

March 18th, 1865

Sir

I have the honour to receive your letter of yesterday's date making inquiries for the information of Mr Secretary Cardwell respecting Mr Duncan, the Director of the Botanic Garden of Mauritius, who has expressed a desire to retire from his duties there, on the ground of his indifferent health etc.

I was made acquainted with his appointment at the time by Earl Grey. As was the practice with the Colonies formerly, they did not care to have well-educated and scientific men in charge of the gardens. It was sufficient if they were kept in a sufficient state for agreeable recreation. In the case in question the Governor asked expressly for a "common but good practical gardener" and Earl Grey sent Mr Duncan to Dr. Lindley to ask how far he considered him likely to answer the purpose of the Governor.

His reply was as mine would have been, if I had been asked, "Quite so." He would well answer the purpose for which he was intended. His predecessor Newman was quite a man of the same stamp. Duncan received his appointment, and by his energy and good conduct did succeed in improving the Garden and grounds to a very great extent; and I believe was rewarded in proportion by an increase of salary and privileges. He carried on a not infrequent correspondence with our Establishment, and there was an interchange of plants mutually advantageous. Beyond mere gardening duties I do not think he aspired. He never was and never could have become a Botanist, nor even what is called a scientific Horticulturist, for want of early education — and I have reason to know there is a general feeling with the Legislature of the Colony that if Duncan were to retire they would cheerfully with the sanction of the Home Government make provision for a very superior man.

Still I candidly confess that Duncan has accomplished more, much more than his warmest friends had expected of him & more than most Gardeners could have done in his rank of the profession.

There[fore] I think he has great merit & is deserving of some indulgence at the hands of the Treasury.

I am etc[9]

With Hooker's backing obtained, the governor was able to recommend that the pension of £147-5-2 to which James was entitled, following a strict interpretation of the rules, should be increased to £198-4-0. At the same time, Barkly agreed that the vacancy should be filled by the 'best qualified scientific Botanist and Horticulturist'. The new salary scale would be £450 to £600 plus expenses, and Barkly proposed that the appointment should be made at the top of the scale which 'may be accomplished without having recourse to the Legislature.' Did the governor, a botanist himself, fear that his colleagues in Port Louis might resist such an enormous increase in salary for James Duncan's replacement? Barkly went on, in his letter to Mr Secretary Cardwell, to say:

> It is but just however to my predecessors in this Government to observe that in Colonial Communities where students of science are few, Botanical Gardens are regarded chiefly as places of amusement and recreation for the public, and as Scientific Botanists are not often practical cultivators or skilful florists, a Gardener accustomed to keep pleasure grounds in order is a matter of prime necessity.

Fortunately, John Horne, the assistant director, could do the gardening job.[10]

Kew proceeded to select Dr Charles Meller for the top position at Pamplemousses. Meller was a young physician and botanist, still aged only thirty, who had travelled with Livingstone on the Zambezi, and had travelled subsequently in Madagascar. Bad health had forced him to return to Britain, where he had joined the staff at Kew. He seems to have been an agreeable man. Sir Walter Besant described him as 'another kindly unbeliever of my acquaintance, who went with a High Church mission to Central Africa, and was one of the few survivors of an unlucky enterprise. He brought with him from Africa a fever which never left him.'[11]

He now accepted the post of director, though Mauritius would seem to have been no place for him to live. He arrived on the island in June 1866, but the following year there was a serious outbreak of malaria. This was followed by an infestation of sugar canes by weevils and in October 1868 Meller was sent on an overseas trip in search of new varieties of sugar cane to combat the weevils. It was on this trip, in February 1869, that he died, in Australia.

131

Following Meller's death, John Horne was promoted after all to the position of director, though not at Meller's salary. The governor pointed out to the Colonial Office that 'a saving of nearly £600 per annum will thus be affected.' In due course, a new assistant director was appointed, named William Scott. He in turn succeeded Horne as director, and the two of them one after the other ran the Garden successfully to almost the end of the century.

18

'A FAVOURITE RESORT'

The fullest account of the Botanic Garden that we have, in the form in which it existed shortly after James left Mauritius, is provided by Nicolas Pike, who was American Consul on the island for five years from January 1867.[1] His *Subtropical Rambles in the Land of the Aphanapteryx* was published seven years after James's departure, by which time many features of the garden had been developed further by Charles Meller and John Horne. However, it seems that Pike wrote the bulk of his account soon after his arrival in Mauritius, and before 1869: he says in a footnote that he wrote the section on the Garden before the death of Dr Meller in Australia, which occurred in that year. His account is probably based largely, therefore, on the Garden as it was just four years after James's departure, and it is a little odd that he does not mention James, nor indeed any other director of the Botanic Garden between Poivre and Meller. One can only conclude that a somewhat skewed account of recent history was given him by Dr Meller. All the same, this must be a fairly accurate description of the gardens as they were in 1865, fifteen years after James Duncan found the wasteland that he described in his first letters to Lord Grey and Sir William Hooker.

Pike starts his tour of what he calls this 'favourite resort of the citizens of Port Louis' at the main entrance, through the newly installed iron gates.

> As far as the eye can reach, a long straight avenue extends, thickly lined on each side with the *Latania glaucophylla* palm (Mauritius), and towering above them to a great height are the slender stems of the areca-nut palm (*Areca catechu*), sometimes, but erroneously, called the Betel nut, with its small tuft of feathery leaves forming its crown. Below these leaves are clusters of bright yellow fruit, which the Indians and Malays chew, with the leaf of the Betel plant (*Piper Chavica*) and lime. This fruit possesses intoxicating properties, and powerfully stimulates the salivary glands and digestive organs, and diminishes the perspiration of the skin.

In the far distance, in the centre of the avenue, is an obelisk, erected to the memory of those who have introduced into Mauritius either useful plants or animals.

Round this monument are some fine specimens of a rare and beautiful palm, the *Latania aurea* (Duncan), from Rodrigues. The natives of that island build their houses with the outer slabs of its trunk; make the rafters of its leaf stalks, which sometimes attain the length of six to ten feet, with a diameter of two to four inches thick, and thatch them with its leaves.

From the obelisk we pass over a little bridge, spanning a clear stream, down a long winding path, so densely shaded by the Traveller's Tree (*Ravenala Madagascariensis*), Vacoas (*Pandanus utilis*), Raffias (*Sagus Ruffia*), and others, that it is impervious to the sun at noonday, and gives a better idea of tropical scenery than any other part of the gardens. Here and there are clumps of the feathery Bamboo, which prettily conceal little pavilions with seats and tables, where you may breakfast or dine quite undisturbed by passers by.

The extension of this walk is bordered with the Stevenson palm (*Stevensonia grandifolia*), and passes the new rosary, where are thousands of rose trees grafted or budded with all the varieties of Europe, except the loveliest of all, the Moss rose, which has either not been introduced, or will not thrive.

There is a small lake, surrounded by a grassy bank, and full of blue and white lotus plants [i.e. water-lilies], that in the season cover its surface with their large blossoms. There are also some fine specimens of the lace, or lattice leaf plant (*Ouvirandra fenestralis*), with its curious skeleton leaves, dichotomous spiked inflorescence, and pretty white flowers which show their heads just above the water.

Further on is a large lake, containing several pretty islands, two of which are approached by bridges, and have seats under the trees for visitors. The centre islands are inaccessible, and are covered with the traveller's tree, palms, casuarinas, and a tangle of flowering shrubs and underwood. There are two fine white swans on its waters, presented by Lady Barkly . . . .

Half encircling this lake is a winding alley of fine sago palms (*Cycas circinalis*), and rare shrubs and flowers are planted between it and the water's edge in clumps in the grass. . . . Terminating the sago walk, rise about a dozen magnificent specimens of *Oreodoxa regia* palm (Cuba), far exceeding in beauty those of the King's Gardens at Rio de Janeiro.

The walk round the other half of this lake, is bordered with rows of the *Licuala horrida* palm, rightly named, for every stem and leaf is bristling with thousands of sharp spines.

In a corner between this lake and the garden wall is a small plantation of the China grass cloth plants (*Boehmeria nivea*), the fibre of which is said to be worth in the European and American markets, about 80l. to 100l. the ton. It is cultivated here as an experiment, for propagation and distribution to the planters.

Pike went on to describe how, on turning to the left on entering the gardens, one came on two walks shaded by magnificent trees, the most remarkable of which he listed: the *Lecythis minor*, with its large fruit in the form of an urn, from which the top spontaneously separates like a lid; the *Bassia latifolia*, or Illipie tree, the fruit of which, when pressed, yields oil used for lamps, soap making and food; the poisonous *Strychnos nux-vomica*, or Strychnine tree; the Camphor tree (*Camphora officinarum*); the *Hymenœa courbaril* and *Hymenœa verrucosa*, used in the planking of vessels; the *Chrysophyllum*, or Star Apple; the *Semecarpus anacardium*, from the seeds of which varnish is obtained; the *Tectona grandis*, or Teak tree; and so on.

The ground under the shade of these interesting trees has recently been laid out in beds for the better cultivation of shade-loving plants, or rather plants that require shade in so hot a climate, such as begonias, fuchias, gloxinias, gesnerias, &c. &c. This pleasant spot is close to another alley of fine palms, arecas of different species, and at intervals are seats, from which a fine view of the Peter Both Mountain is obtained. Many of these palms are 100 years old. Sad destruction was made among them by the hurricane of March 1868, and as it would take a great amount of time and labour to replace the old trees by young ones, and the soil would require entirely renovating, mahogany trees are being planted in their places. . . .

In the centre of the gardens, a portion of ground is set apart for a nursery. This produces a large supply of young plants for distribution in the colony. In 1865 over 50,000 young trees were distributed. New varieties of the sugar-cane are also propagated in this nursery, to enable the planters to replace the exhausted varieties now cultivated in the island.

To the right of the main entrance are rows of new exotics and beds of bright-coloured flowers and shrubs, all classified and named. Beyond these is one of the pleasantest parts of the gardens; a grassy slope extending downwards to another large lake, that has also a pretty island encircled with rock work, Raffias and Vacoas. . . .

Out of this lake flows a stream, with a pretty fall of water that passes under an iron bridge into the ravine below.

A very attractive feature on the grassy slope is a gigantic baobab (*Adansonia digitata*), measuring thirty feet around at the collum. . . . Scattered over the turf is a small collection of coniferous trees, natives of both hemispheres. Many of them have only been planted about three or four years, but they would scarcely be excelled in beauty in their own climates.

There are very fine specimens of araucarias, dammaras, pinus, two or three specimens of thujas, cupressus, juniperus, and callitris. . . .

In the midst of all this wealth of tropical vegetation, here and there one starts with delight, as one finds some of our northern climate's pet flowers. Close to the monstrous Baobab is a bed where the English honeysuckle blooms in wild profusion, and most of us are tempted to break the strict rules against gathering flowers, in order to take away a spray that recalls so vividly 'auld lang syne.' Passing along the upper part of the grassy slope, over a stone bridge, covered with the large blue thunbergia, you see the cottage of the sub-director on the left, with the chief's offices. . . .

In a pretty enclosure on the right is the house of Dr. Meller, the Director of the Gardens, with its verandah completely hidden behind masses of the lilac bourgainvillæa, the scarlet ipomæa, and monster passion flowers. . . .

Close to Dr. Meller's house is the Fernery, admirably situated on a rocky descent, with a pretty sparkling stream at its foot. It contains many hundreds of ferns and orchids, about 150 of which are natives of Mauritius. Here may be seen the celebrated Coco de mer, from Seychelles, with its great twin nuts . . .

It would be a hopeless task to try and give a more detailed account of all the beautiful trees, shrubs, creepers, &c., of these gardens, as there is no printed guide to them, and except the late additions none are named, so that it is an *embarras de richesses* when one attempts a description of them.

Pike's description of the gardens is so detailed, that a rewarding exercise is to follow his route, with the aim of identifying so far as is possible what is the same, what has changed, and how the Garden has developed over the past 150 years. What follows, therefore, is an account of a walk through the Garden, Pike's book in hand, one hot and humid day in February 2005.

The white iron gates, smart and freshly painted, but no longer new, still stand at the entrance. (This is undoubtedly the best way into the garden, although most visitors now enter via the car park to the north, up Mon Plaisir Avenue, across lawns and through former orchards that were not part of the Botanic Garden in the 1860s.) Leading directly away from the gates, Labourdonnais Avenue still stretches as far as the eye can see, lined even more densely than before with palms and forest trees competing in height for the light that filters through the canopy.

The Liénard obelisk stands at the same crossing, but a number of names have been added to it since the first were carved in 1861. One of the first was that of Charles Meller himself, added soon after his death, in 1869, in spite of the brief period he was director of the garden. His predecessor, James Duncan, and his successor, John Horne, had to wait over a hundred years until their names were added to the south face of the obelisk in 1979. Working gardeners, as both of them were, they may have impressed their fellow Victorians less than the gentleman botanist, Dr Charles Meller. The latest name to be added is that of Nicolas Pike, whose account of the garden we are now following.

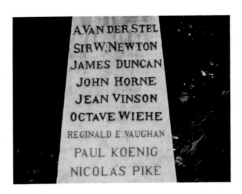

According to Pike, the monument was surrounded by 'a rare and beautiful Palm, the *Latania aurea* (Duncan), from Rodrigues'. Some of these 'yellow lattans' are still the most prominent trees surrounding the obelisk, though because James Duncan's name for them (which Pike took from his *Catalogue*) was never validly published, the correct name today is *Latania verschaffeltii* Lemaire.

Walking on, past the long rectangular pond with its splendid display of Amazon water-lilies, which was not mentioned by Pike, perhaps because in his time it was still a fish tank (the lilies were introduced later), one still passes over a bridge, which crosses a small canal, after which there is a choice of 'winding paths' leading to Stevenson Avenue, named after James's favourite governor. In Pike's day this walk was already lined with the palm which James had written to Hooker about in September 1859, wanting to name it *Stevensonia grandifolia*. Alas, this palm, which comes from the Seychelles, had in fact been earlier described, and therefore it goes today by the name *Phoenicophorium borsigianum* (K.Koch) Stuntz.[2] Nevertheless, it, or rather its descendents, still line the avenue, and a handsome tree it is.

What came next for Pike, but is no longer there, was 'the new rosary', with its thousands of rose trees. This was one of Meller's favourite developments, a rosary, in his words, 'between the long and round lakes', where he cleared the ground of 'scrub and useless trees'. Today, the trees are back.

Next comes the lotus pond, just as it did for Pike, its surface covered by the white Asian lotus, with water-lilies of different colours growing in the surrounding irrigation canals. Beyond it is the much larger Grand Bassin, Pike's 'large lake', which James had made out of swampy land at the northern extremity of the garden at that time. It is a delightful spot, still looking as it did in Pike's time. Two of the islands, accessible by bridge, have kiosks which provide shade and seating for visitors. The other islands, which are inaccessible, appear to be quite wild, though in fact the thick growth requires careful control, work carried out successfully by the present director in recent years.

Pike then returns to the entrance gates, and describes two avenues to the left of the entrance 'shaded by magnificent trees'. These must be the lengthy Céré and Paul et Virginie Avenues, running parallel to the main road outside the garden, for some of the species described by Pike are still to be found along these walks. Perhaps not the same trees; but there are still some ancient trees nearby, such as the *Diospyros tesselaria*, the Mauritian ebony, which may be the oldest tree in the garden.

Next to these avenues, however, where Pike found beds 'recently' laid out for begonias, gloxinias and so on, there has been a complete change. A rectangular grid of avenues named after 19th century directors – Duncan, Meller, Horne, Scott – and lined with palms (and crotons in the case of Duncan Avenue) has replaced the bedding plants. Indeed, it is possible that without the 'rows of new exotics and beds of bright-coloured flowers and shrubs' the garden in the time of James Duncan was actually closer in appearance to what we see today, than it was during Pike's visit when the borders so beloved by the mid-Victorians were freshly planted. Pike seems to have had broad tastes in garden design, but he was a man of his time, as can be seen by his reference to the romantic bed of honeysuckles.

Apart from these borders, also replaced by this rectangular grid of trees was almost certainly the nursery, from which 50,000 young plants were distributed annually throughout the island.

To complete his tour, Pike described what he encountered on turning right as he entered the gates of the Garden. He described this as 'one of the pleasantest parts of the gardens', and many people feel the same way about it today, even though it is the least visited area, and part of it, 'Le Petit Jardin', was sold by John Newman to the government for incorporation within the Garden only shortly before James arrived in Mauritius.

There have been two major structural changes to this section of the Garden, both of which can be seen in the plan of Pamplemousses drawn by James's son James William in 1859 in his capacity as assistant government surveyor. Although it is a plan of the village, not the Botanic Garden, this part of the Garden is included in it.

Firstly, when James arrived, what is now Poivre Avenue was a public road, made necessary in the early 19th century by the collapse of the bridge on the main road over the Citron River. The inconvenience of having an unfenced public road cutting the Garden in two was a constant bugbear of James's early days, and it was not until Stevenson Bridge was opened in 1864 that the Garden could be closed off and its plants properly protected. Pike visited the Garden not long after this happened, by which time Poivre Avenue had become the delightful curved walk, lined with royal palms, that we see today.

Secondly, Pike described a lake with an island and a waterfall which no longer exist. This lake had been formed by damming the river, but following the malaria epidemic of 1867-68 the lake was drained. Today the river flows at the bottom of its steep sided valley unhindered. Two flights of stone steps were built by James to link Poivre Avenue with Adrien d'Epinay Avenue, which runs parallel to it and which used to run along the shore of the lake. Today there is planting right down to the river, which is really a stream, except when in full spate.

But to return to the planting. Pike's gigantic baobab still stands, near an avenue of bottle palms (*Hyophorbe lagenicaulis*) from Round Island, one of James's introductions to the Garden. Beyond, the 'newly planted' coniferous trees have reached magnificent heights. Pike suggests that the trees he saw were only three or four years old, but given that all the specimens he lists were, according to the *Catalogue*, introduced by James, it is likely that they were in fact somewhat older at that time.

Pike then describes how, passing along the top of a grassy slope, and over a stone bridge, one comes to the sub-director's house and the 'offices'. He would have walked along what is now called Octave Wiéhé Avenue and over Le Pont des Soupirs. This is a most handsome construction, from which one can look down to the river at the bottom of the valley. There are indeed today the ruins of buildings beyond the bridge, a picturesque sight with bougainvillea and creepers climbing through the roofless walls. Was one of these John Horne's cottage? It seems possible, resembling as it does the plan sketched by the engineer who costed the proposals in James's letter of 24th November 1860.

The exact location of the house of the director himself is more of a mystery. Pike describes it as being 'in a pretty enclosure on the right.' It is probable that he is describing the approach to the bridge, which would place the house on the flat ground between the bridge and the main road, near where there is still a minor entrance to the Garden. A.W. Owadally, author of the excellent guide book to the Botanic Garden, points out that iron hinges are still visible on the pillars at the west end of the bridge, and that these mark the gate which led to the Director's house, the former nursery and the fernery. This gate would have been necessary at the period when the avenue beyond the bridge was a public road.[3]

Close examination of the site could not reveal any trace of the house, which was a wooden structure. But half hidden by undergrowth are stone terraces, with steps leading down the steep slope to the river, and this must be the site of the fernery. Meller, in his report of 1866, said that he had made a new fernery, which was formerly 'too closely congregated in an inconspicuous and inconvenient spot.' One cannot say whether the romantic site that exists today was the original fernery or was Meller's later version – one suspects the former, planted near James's house where he could have kept an eye on it.

19

EPILOGUE

So James and Sarah returned to Britain. Fifteen years after he had left, James would have found many changes. His father William and his mentor Sir William Hooker were both dead. The Great Exhibition of 1851 was now many years in the past and the Crystal Palace, designed by that other gardener Joseph Paxton, who had supposedly used the leaf structure of the Amazon water-lily as his inspiration for the building, had been moved to south London. Charles Darwin had published, in 1859, *The Origin of Species*, and religious certainty was changing to doubt as a prevailing mood. The writing of one of the most popular expressions of late Victorian doubt, Matthew Arnold's *Dover Beach*, coincided with James's time in Mauritius: drafted in 1851, it was first published in 1867.

> The Sea of Faith
> Was once, too, at the full and round earth's shore
> Lay like the folds of a bright girdle furl'd.
> But now I only hear
> Its melancholy, long, withdrawing roar,
> Retreating, to the breath
> Of the night-wind, down the vast edges drear
> And naked shingles of the world.

Though it is perhaps unlikely that James would have appreciated these sentiments, given what seem to have been his straightforward manner and conventional religious views.

Material conditions of life were improving. British cities had begun to introduce vast modern drainage schemes, leading to a general improvement in public health and to the removal of cholera as a threat.

James's social standing must have changed. He left Britain as a gardener, he returned as director of a Royal Botanic Garden. An undated letter from Lord

Grey written from 13 Carlton House Terrace was probably delivered not long after his return to Britain:

Duncan

I send you an order of admission to see the House of Lords & which you can use any Saturday that is convenient to you — we were very glad to see you & your wife again yesterday. The weather is so very cold that you and Mrs Duncan must be very careful after so many years in such a different climate — I have been looking over the catalogue & am quite astonished at the number of plants you have added to the garden —

We shall be glad to see you again some day that you may be in London.

Yours faithfully

H Grey[1]

There is a question now to be addressed, which is how wealthy was James in his retirement? And what was the source of his money? Throughout his time in Mauritius, he complained that his salary was too low for the job he was being asked to do, and external evidence would seem to indicate that indeed his salary was modest for what was a colony with high living expenses. Yet he did have some capital of his own, as he indicated in a letter to Sir William Hooker of March 1861:

You may remember that when I came out here on a salary of £250 per annum, I was obliged to pay my own passage, and although I had good interest all that I could get from the Government was half salary during the time I was at sea, which didnot [amount] to much. . . . .

I hope no advantage of the delay will be taken to reduce the Salary, which as you must be well aware I fought hard to get established on the scale of from £200 to £300, for as you truly observe I well know what it is to live here, and if I had not had some private means of my own when I came here, I don't know what would have become of my family — only fancy I hade to pay £5 each per month for their education at the Royal College, in Port Louis. Now the case is different, as both my sons earn about £300 per annum each, so much for giving them a good education.[2]

I have been unable to discover where this capital had come from. Was it acquired in the 1830s, before James went to Howick? It did not come from his father, for the letter from John Ferguson of 14th December 1860 made it clear that

William Duncan shortly before his death was not well off and, moreover, was £150 in debt to his son. Yet before his departure from Mauritius, James was in a position to acquire property in Port Louis. His will, dated 23rd June 1873, refers to his 'immoveable property situate at the corner of Rempart and Barrack Street in the Town of Port Louis Mauritius'. (Rempart Street has since been renamed Edith Cavel Street.) This would seem to have been worth as much as £10,000, or over half a million pounds at today's values. James's elder son James William, wrote decades later, on 6th June 1902, to the family's agent in Mauritius, Pier Edmond de Chazal, about this property:

> You will remember that when my father first came home he received £100 a month from that property. . . . [soon after he bought it] he spent a great deal in improving and adding to the buildings which greatly improved and increased the value of the property. . . . I do not know if you remember that when my father left Mauritius he was offered £10,000 for it by an Arab Merchant and declined that offer.[3]

Whether the 'private means' referred to by James in his letter to Hooker, which he already had when he came out from Britain in 1849, was sufficient to buy this property must remain a mystery. There is one conceivable way in which additional capital might have been acquired during the years spent in Mauritius. McCracken, in his *Gardens of Empire*, claims that to compensate for low salaries and to boost the general revenue of botanic gardens, many curators were allowed to sell surplus plant stock to the public, a practice that was commonplace in South African botanic gardens.[4] Pamplemousses, in the absence of commercial nurserymen in Mauritius, was the main supplier of plants to the general public and it would not have been surprising if recipients had made some sort of payment for them. James's own son, John Corbett, was a beneficiary.[5] But there appears to be no mention of payments by the general public for plants in the accounts. For the time being at least, all this remains a mystery.

From London, where they initially lived on their return to Britain, James and Sarah moved to Harrow Weald, and then to West Coker House, near Yeovil in Somerset. A telegram exists which was sent there by their daughter Caroline on 23rd September 1867, announcing her ship's landfall in Plymouth and her impending disembarkation in Southampton the following day.

It must have been soon after Caroline's arrival (with her daughter but without husband) that the only two photographs of James known to exist were taken. The photographs were posed in the open air, it would seem at the edge of

a field, with trees and shrubs out of focus behind the figures, who had clearly been told not to look at the camera. Wearing pale trousers and waistcoat, a dark jacket, and a cravat wound tightly round his neck, and carrying a wide brimmed hat in his hand, James stood nonchalantly among his family: Sarah, John Corbett and Frances Maria, their children George and Caroline, and John Corbett's sister Caroline with her daughter Lilly Sarah. James William was probably still in Mauritius, though he was soon to follow the rest of the family back to Britain – his wife Mary came from Yeovil, so there may be a connection between her and the fact that other members of the family were living in West Coker at the time.

James retained his connections with Mauritius, for according to the Dictionary of Mauritian Biography, in 1871, while he was staying in Newbury, Berkshire, he wrote to recommend 32 different sorts of trees for planting in Mauritius.[6] By 1875 James and Sarah had made their way to Calne, Wiltshire, where they lived at Beaumont Villa, Lickhill Road, an address recorded in that year's Kelly's Directory.[7] Their choice of Calne may be the result of a link which otherwise would be only a striking coincidence. The Vicar of Calne at the time was the Revd John Duncan, from Aberdeen. It is possible that there was a family connection between the two men: the odds must be somewhat against two

Aberdonian Duncans arriving quite independently in a small town in Wiltshire. John Duncan was Vicar of Calne from 1865 to 1907 and was clearly popular, to judge by the report of his large funeral procession. Perhaps he played a part in James's grandson George's decision to enter holy orders.

James himself died in 1876, on 11th August. He was buried at Holy Trinity church, though his gravestone may date from twenty years later, following Sarah's death. The new churchyard of Holy Trinity had replaced that of the mediaeval parish church of St Mary as Calne's parish graveyard, following the building of Holy Trinity in the 1850s by the predecessor of the Revd John Duncan.

The gravestone reads:

IN AFFECTIONATE REMEMBRANCE OF
JAMES DUNCAN
FOR MANY YEARS DIRECTOR OF
THE BOTANICAL GARDENS MAURITIUS
BORN NEAR ABERDEEN IN
OCTOBER 1802
DIED AT CALNE WILTS IN AUGUST 1876
AGED 73 YEARS
AND
SARAH, HIS WIDOW
WHO DIED 3RD AUGUST 1894

AT HIGH WYCOMBE, BUCKS,
AND IS INTERRED HERE
AGED 83 YEARS
AND NOW, LORD, WHAT IS MY HOPE TRULY MY
HOPE IS EVEN IN THEE

PSALM XXXIX V.8

John Corbett with his family had followed his parents to Calne, and he had certainly by then fully reverted to the original family business, for his address in Calne was The Nursery, Curzon Street. In the 1881 census John Corbett's son George, who was by then aged 20, described himself as a 'nurseryman's son'.

After James's death, Sarah left Calne to go to live with her daughter. Caroline had married a second time, this time to a Jonathan Gourley Scott, from Old Machar, Aberdeen.[8] The Scotts were living at 17 Townsend Villa, Richmond, but they later moved to Loakes House, High Wycombe, where Sarah died on 3rd August 1894. She was buried in Calne. The *Daily News* recorded on 9th August the death of the 'widow of James Duncan Director of the Botanical Gardens, Mauritius'.

That same year, James William presented to Kew the 85 drawings of plants recorded as having been made by him when he was a child in Mauritius. He was then living just down the road from Kew, in Twickenham, Middlesex. According to the *Kew Bulletin*,

> In consequence of the great extension of cultivation, many of the rare native plants are extinct, and common ones have become rare. Many of the drawings are figures of orchids, of which we possess only very indifferent specimens, or none at all. The fact that they are localised also adds to their value. Among other rare plants represented are:- *Mussænda Stadtmanni*, *Nuxia verticillata* and *Arndtia mauritiana*.[9]

They are the work of an amateur, not of a professional illustrator, but they make one regret that the collection of his brother George's drawings has not survived. It was George, after all, who was, according to his father, named 'The Young Naturalist'.

In the 1881 census James William described himself as a retired civil servant of Mauritius. His brother John Corbett died in 1899, in Little Perdiswell, near Worcester, where he is buried, leaving James William as the last member of the

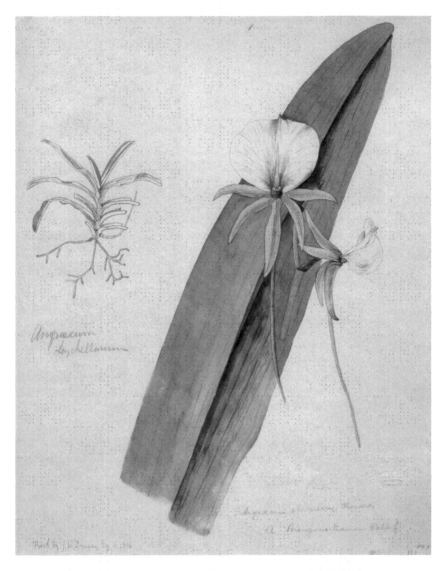

family to have first hand adult memories of Mauritius. On 3rd August 1914, a fateful day, James William wrote to Pier Edmond de Chazal's son André, who had taken over the business at 35 Church Street, Port Louis on the death of his father.

Maidenhead

3 August 1914

Dear Mr de Chazal

From your letter sent me some time ago I have been expecting the very sad news contained in your letter of the 29th. June last, such news as the death of your lamented Father must cause a terrible shock, even though expected, and I beg to tender my very deepest sympathy with your Mother, yourself and all your family – Your father was one of my oldest friends, we were boys together, and spent many happy days together – In July last I spent my seventy ninth birthday and am therefore about two years his senior in age but I am never well lately and I think it will not be very long before I am called upon to follow him to that bourne from which no traveller returns -

I am very much obliged to you for your kind promise to do your best to look after our interests in Mauritius, as your dear Father has done for so many years, and what he wrote to me you would be sure to do. I am the only one of the family left who knows personally anything about the property there and I would be very glad if you could find a Purchaser for it before my decease, and I think all the family are of that opinion – I am also much obliged for permission to use your telegraphic address Mizpah if necessary.

You will be sorry to see by the papers that a general European War has commenced, Austria and Servia, Russia and Germany France are all at War and it is feared that England and others will have to join.

I remain with kindest regards & deepest sympathy with all your family,

Yours ever truly

JWD[10]

James William died the following year, in 1915.

A Botanist's Comments

James Duncan's Catalogue of Plants in the Royal Botanical Garden, Mauritius

H.J. Noltie, Royal Botanic Garden Edinburgh

Lists have a certain appeal to those with a mind of a particular bent – it is not so much the dry material itself, as the associations and reflections they evoke or inspire. Even such an ostensibly purely functional list as a telephone directory is not devoid of interest, including as it does personal names and addresses in addition to the numbers that are its primary purpose. These can lead to observations and speculations on correlations of names with geography (residues of clan systems), the ubiquity of some surnames and rarity of others, and, for snobs, social information such as associations between particular addresses and people with titles or double-barrelled names. Botanical lists, though appearing equally arid at first sight, are far more informative than phone books, once one knows how to read them. Duncan's is a case in point. It provides remarkably similar categories of information to a phone book – family names, specific names (in binomial form: generic noun and specific epithet), the name of the person who described and named the plant (its 'author', usually off-puttingly abbreviated), and even the equivalent of an 'address' in the source of origin of the plant. That such catalogues are so much more interesting than phone books is largely because of the fascinating mechanism of botanical nomenclature, with its complicated set of rules, dating back to Linnaeus in the eighteenth century, defining how plants are to be named. When a name is published that of its author is appended to the binomial so that it can be traced to its source, where information on where the plant was first found, and by whom, is usually given. This process has been made much easier since an intervention by Charles Darwin, who left money in his will so that his friend Sir Joseph Hooker could organise the compilation of a list of all then known plant names and their place of publication, the work being undertaken by Benjamin Daydon Jackson. The first volume of this list *par excellence*, the *Index Kewensis*, first appeared in 1893, but has been kept updated to this day, and in 1997 contained 989,492 names. (It is now available on the internet via 'IPNI'). With the help of this supremely useful 'finding aid', the reader can flesh out the bare bones of Duncan's initially bleak *Catalogue*, together with material added from his own stock of knowledge of the history of plant discoveries, plant biogeography, the biographies of plant collectors and authors, the names they coined and applied … and so forth.

The *Catalogue of Plants in the Royal Botanical Garden, Mauritius* provides a fascinating picture of a colonial garden at a particular window in time, 1863. Moreover it concerns a garden that (partly because of its geographical position between the Cape of Good Hope, India and Australia) played a significant role in the network of such organisations centred on the eponymous organisation at Kew. These gardens were microcosms of botanical biodiversity containing plants from the furthest corners of the world, and even a mere listing of their contents can lead to tales of plant exploration and description, man's use of plants, and the transfer of botanical benefits across the globe. Such gardens, particularly on a small island, also had important local social and practical agri-horticultural roles: in propagating ornamental and useful plants for private gardens, and acclimatising new introductions or breeding new forms for the benefit of local farmers and agricultural industries. A further role of these gardens was scientific – as a base for exploration of the local flora, though in Duncan's case this seems to have been limited. Although he introduced many plants to his garden 'from the [local] Forests', and sent living material (seeds and plants) to John Smith at Kew, Duncan seems to have sent few or any herbarium specimens for delectation and study by European taxonomists and had not the expertise to undertake taxonomic work himself. In fact by this stage there was rather little left on Mauritius in the way of novelties to be described, largely as a result of extensive French exploration in the eighteenth century – the exception being some palms to which I will return.

While this *Catalogue* is typical of its genre, it is certainly impressive in the range of material grown, in terms of taxonomic and geographical scope. One organisational aspect, however, makes it hard to use botanically, and reflects Duncan's horticultural (rather than 'scientific') background. The list is arranged alphabetically by generic, rather than family, name, so that related genera are widely separated, making it harder to discover, for example, particular interests of Duncan's. It contains numerous spelling or typographical errors, which would most certainly not have been approved of by European botanical pundits such as the punctilious Hookers of Kew, and is entirely devoid of supplementary notes on species. Duncan claimed his *Catalogue* to be the first to list the species growing at Pamplemousses (Preface: [i] 'no work of the kind previously existed'), and while it is the first exclusively devoted to the garden, the statement is slightly disingenuous and could, perhaps, be taken as a slur on his predecessor Wenceslas (a.k.a. Wenzel) Bojer. Duncan certainly knew of Bojer's *Hortus Mauritianus* of 1837, in which are listed the native and introduced plants of the whole island, but those growing in the 'jardin du Roi, Pampl.' are specifically noted. Bojer's work, like Duncan's, contains no plant descriptions (even of the novelties for which he coined new names); numerous natural and garden localities are cited and it is arranged (more usefully) according to the Candollean natural system. As Baker (1877: 9) pointed out, Bojer's work is unusually useful for discriminating native from introduced species, something that would have been much harder to do in later years.

In Duncan's *Catalogue* some 2385 taxa are recognised at species level or below (i.e., including varieties and cultivars) though by no means all are named, and Duncan commented in his Preface that many of the recent introductions 'have probably never been described by any Botanist'. Two examples of named species from India show how relatively quickly plants with very restricted wild distributions could move around and become established in cultivation – both the spectacular creeper *Hexacentris* (now *Thunbergia*) *mysorensis* from the Western Ghats, and the palm *Livistona jenkinsiana* from upper Assam, were described only in 1845 but were growing at Pamplemousses by 1863. Duncan was quite rightly keen to show how immensely hard he had worked in his (by then) 14 years as Superintendent, annotating those he had personally introduced '(a)' – an astonishing 1464 taxa, representing 61% of the total list.

As there are no notes in the *Catalogue*, the only way of discovering more about the plants listed is by looking up their original descriptions, located by means of *Index Kewensis*. This works only for published names, and the list includes many that were floating around in horticultural circles such as nursery or botanic garden catalogues, but never validly published with a description (or if so, then under different names). Doing this reveals a surprising amount, though it has been possible only to sample some that appeared potentially interesting, especially ones recently described in Duncan's time by authors such as W.J. Hooker, John Lindley, Joseph Paxton, and, in the case of palms, by Hermann Wendland. Species described by older authors such as Linnaeus, Willdenow and De Candolle are likely to have been long in cultivation, and of lesser interest in this context. Targetting the former group, a picture emerges of plants arriving at Pamplemousses mainly through the horticultural trade and from other botanic gardens, and there is nothing to suggest direct contacts with any of the major plant collectors of the period. Even introduction of plants from the Cape of Good Hope and Australia, which might have been expected to have been direct, on grounds of geography and trade routes, seems largely to have been via Europe, being of well established horticultural plants. There remains the possibility of direct links with India, through Calcutta, and even smaller gardens such as that of the Agri-Horticultural Society of Madras, but this is hard to pin down from the *Catalogue* and its names alone.

A tenuous connection with the Royal Botanic Garden Edinburgh was uncovered while perusing the list, and one that is not generally known, though the link is indirect as the plant concerned '*Poinsettia* (now *Euphorbia*) *pulcherrima* Grah.' had already been in cultivation for 25 years by Duncan's time. It is interesting to note that this ubiquitous Christmas potplant, now widely established as a weed in the tropics, was first described from specimens flowering at the RBGE in 1836 by the Garden's Regius Keeper, Robert Graham. [The connection with Isaac Bayley Balfour over Duncan's palms (see below), is similarly indirect as it dates from the period before he became Regius Keeper of Edinburgh.]

Links with Kew and the Horticultural Society (later RHS) prove as strong as expected, but what is more surprising are the large number of plants associated with the Belgian horticultural trade, especially that of Ghent, and firms such as Verschaffelt – and not only for palms. Two of the plant names can be associated with other European botanic gardens – *Caladium picturatum* appeared in a seed list of the Berlin Botanic Garden and *Stadmannia giesbrechtii* in one from Naples – it is possible that these came about through direct gift or exchange, but they could equally well have arrived via London.

Geographical range

It is of some interest to analyse the sources of Duncan's plants, though this cannot be complete as they are not always given. And in any case, as already pointed out, most were not imported directly from their original homes.

India (including Nepal, Burma & Ceylon): 366 (= 22.5%)

Mauritius & Rodrigues: 321 (= 19.8%)

South America: 182 (= 11.2%)

SE Asia (including the Indonesian Islands and Indo-China): 136 (= 8.4%)

Central America and the West Indies: 125 (= 7.7%)

Australia & Oceania (including New Zealand
& the South Sea Islands): 109 (= 6.7%)

China & Japan: 96 (= 5.9%)

Madagascar & the Indian Ocean Islands (excepting Mauritius
& Rodrigues): 96 (= 5.9%)
Cape of Good Hope & Natal: 65 (= 4%)
Europe, Mediterranean, Levant and Arabia: 62 (= 3.8%)
Africa (except South Africa): 51 (= 3.1%)
North America (temperate): 15 (= 0.9%)

In many ways the most interesting botanically would be those from Mauritius itself, were only some additional information given. Many of these were doubtless endemics including some of the palms and screw pines (*Pandanus* spp.), but in the absence of further details or voucher specimens one cannot be certain of the accuracy of their identification; or what the ones merely denoted 'species' eventually turned out to be. As already noted, the majority of Mauritian species were known by this date, collected by naturalist-explorers such as Commerson, Bory de Saint Vincent and Du Petit Thouars, and described by themselves, or by Paris-based botanists such as Lamarck.

The largest external source of plants for Duncan's garden proves, perhaps not surprisingly, to be India, and it would be interesting to know more about his links with the gardens of Calcutta, Madras and Ceylon. Although many of these plants were in general tropical circulation by 1863, given their large representation at Pamplemousses, the ease of transport and frequency of communication between the two 'colonies', to say nothing of the large Indian community in the garden (coolie labour) and Mauritius itself, extensive direct horticultural communication must almost certainly have been taking place. However, as a warning one could take the example of *Meyenia hawtayneana*. The source 'Neelgherries' initially suggested a direct import from the Madras Presidency, but on further investigation the plant is found to have been sent thence by Wallich to the Duke of Northumberland at Syon as early as the 1820s, and it was in general cultivation by 1840.

The second largest 'exotic' element is from South America, and doubtless merely represents the strengths of Duncan's links with London (Kew and the Horticultural Society) and Belgium.

Duncan had some contacts with Ferdinand von Mueller in Melbourne, though only two eucalypts and the conifer *Dammara* (now *Agathis*) *robusta* can be linked directly with him. The remaining Australian species had been in cultivation from earlier times and originated largely in New South Wales rather than Victoria, through Duncan's direct contacts with Sydney. *Araucaria bidwillii*, the bunya-bunya pine, is of interest: it was not in cultivation when first described by Hooker in 1843, a deficiency evidently made up over the following 20 years, but whether or not this was through direct contact with Australia is unknown. The cycad *Catakidozamia macleayi* was not formally described until 1869, by Miquel in Amsterdam, but the name was clearly in circulation before this – and here is another probable introduction via a nursery in the Low Countries.

Taxonomic range

Some families are especially well represented in the *Catalogue*, and suggest special interests on Duncan's part, notably palms (177 taxa), orchids (99) and ferns/clubmosses (125). Others are well represented merely because they belong to big families with large numbers of useful members (e.g., Leguminosae).

The palm collection is noteworthy. Many were at this date only recently described, especially through the exertions of Hermann Wendland (1825–1903), with epithets showing them to have been introduced into cultivation through the Belgian nursery trade: e.g. *Chamaedorea lindeniana*, *C. verschaffeltii*, *Chamaerops ghiesbreghtii*, *Geonoma ghiesbreghtiana*, *G. verschaffeltii*.

Useful plants

On close examination of the list there are slightly fewer economically useful species than one would have expected; though perhaps by 1863 this function of botanic gardens was already in decline. For example, there are notably few grasses – a few bamboos and only a single species (*Panicum maximum*) of the group one would have expected as being tried as fodder crops. In fact the majority of the non-Mauritian species on the list are ornamentals.

Nonetheless one can point to some interesting economic species under various headings.

Medicinal: *Adhatoda vasica*, *Castanospermum australe* (now known to have anti-HIV and anti-cancer properties) and *Cassia fistula*.

Timber trees both temperate and tropical: this category doubtless accounts for the surprisingly large number of conifers, including *Cryptomeria japonica*, '*Dacrydium spicatum*' (an unpublished name attributed to Joseph Hooker), five species of *Araucaria*, three of *Thuja*. It was probably as potential timber (or at least firewood) trees, that six each of eucalypts and she-oaks (*Casuarina* spp.), were grown. Satinwood and teak are not surprising, but the English oak had presumably been introduced by one of Duncan's predecessors for reasons of nostalgia.

Raw materials: sugar cane; scented oils (*Anatherum muticum*, *Andropogon schoenanthus*, patchouli); dyes (*Bixa orellana*, *Memecylon tinctoria*, *Haemotoxylum campechianum*); fibres (*Agave* spp., cotton, jute – *Corchorus* spp.), mulberries (as hosts for silkworms), the rice-paper plant (*Aralia papyrifera*), *Boehmeria nivea*, the Panama hat plant (*Carludovica palmata*) and flaxes both European and New Zealand.

Foods: pot herbs (*Amaranthus oleraceus*, *Basella alba*); tubers (*Amorphophallus campanulatus*, *Batatas edulis*, manioc); beverages (coffee, maté tea); cereals (*Zea mays*, *Paspalum scrobiculatum*); legumes (*Cajanus* spp., the ground nut and a local speciality 'Pois [mis-spelt 'Bois'!] Noire', *Mucuna utilis*); spices (cinnamon, black pepper, cardamom, chilis (four varieties), cloves, star anise, and even European mint and thyme).

Fruits: a respectable collection of citrus, and a large one (25) of named mango varieties; bananas; pineapples (five varieties); star fruit; and the usual tropical ones such as pawpaw and guava.

Vegetables: as demonstrated by the oak tree, expatriates seemed to suffer from homesickness that could be alleviated botanically: in addition to various tropical species, garlic, onions and leeks make appearances!

Ornamentals

As already stated a large proportion of plants on the list are more or less purely ornamental. Duncan seems to have had an obsession for roses, growing no fewer than 197 varieties! Nostalgia again, for there are few sadder horticultural sights than the attempt to grow roses in tropical climes, where they never achieve anything approaching full rosehood. Much more suitable were the 'upwards of two hundred very distinct varieties' of the 'Amaryllis', now botanically *Hippeastrum*, dubbed by Duncan the 'Tulip of the Tropics'. As in Victorian gardens back home Duncan was keen on flowering shrubs: temperate ones such as camellias (12 cultivars), rhododendrons (12 cultivars of the Japanese '*Azalea indica*'), and the more gaudy tropical ixoras and lagerstroemias. There are many cacti, and other Victorian favourites such as 'chrysanthemums' (four varieties) and plants with decorative foliage such as begonias and caladiums. Central and South American members of the family Gesneriaceae are also conspicuous: gloxinias (14) and achimenes (13 cultivars).

Also of interest are what might be termed 'trophy plants' such as the palm that produces the largest of all known seeds, the coco de mer (*Lodoicea maldivica*). In this context the giant waterlily (*Victoria amazonica*), though known to have been cultivated by Duncan earlier on, is notable by its absence from the list. But two spectacular leguminous trees also fall into this category: *Amherstia nobilis* and *Poinciana* (now *Delonix*) *regia*. *Amherstia*, the 'orchid tree', was first collected in Burma by Nathaniel Wallich, named by him after his friend

Lady Amherst, wife of the Governor-General of India, and distributed by him from the Calcutta Botanic Garden. *Delonix*, the flamboyant, now one of the most popular of tropical street trees worldwide came originally from Madagascar, but Pamplemousses played an important role in its introduction into cultivation. It was first discovered in Madagascar by Duncan's predecessor Bojer, who sent a description and excellent drawing of it (by himself) to W.J. Hooker in Glasgow, who published it in 1829 in the *Botanical Magazine* in which so many of the plants grown by Duncan made their first appearance.

Curiosities that must have been favourites to botanically curious visitors to Pamplemousses include the baobab (with its monstrously swollen trunk), the tortoise-like woody corm of the elephant's foot yam (*Testudinaria* (now *Dioscorea*) *eliphantipes*), and the lace-like leaves of the submerged aquatic *Ouvirandra* (now *Aponogeton*) *fenestrale*.

There is a downside to botanical translocations, and this is when a species becomes invasive when moved to a different locality. The *Catalogue* provides one example of this – the daisy *Parthenium hysterophorus*. No longer would this be treasured in a botanical garden! Originating in North America it has become a widespread tropical weed, and whilst not a major problem in terms of space occupied, it is a menace as in some people it evokes an extremely nasty (even fatal) allergic dermatitis.

Duncan as a taxonomist

The *Catalogue* is devoid of descriptions, so names coined therein are '*nomina nuda*' and not validly published (for a name to be validly published it must be accompanied by a description, or refer to an already published one). Isaac Bayley Balfour (who wrote the account of the palm family in Baker's *Flora of Mauritius*) came to the rescue, however, and adopted Duncan's suggested name of *Stevensonia* for a palm genus, with the single species *S. grandifolia*. Technically these are Balfour's names, though for reasons of botanical courtesy are cited as 'Duncan ex Balf. f.', so Duncan makes a small appearance as a botanical author, even though neither genus nor species is still recognised, both having earlier validly published names. However, an interesting story of botanical skulduggery emerges over the correct name for the genus: *Phoenicophorium*. This was published by Wendland in the Belgian journal *L'Illustration Horticole* in 1865. Although Wendland was aware of Duncan's suggested generic name, as it was not validly published he was not actually obliged to use it (though to have done so would have been polite!) However, when giving the name *Phoenicophorium sechellarum* to the species, Wendland said this was the same as the earlier name

Astrocaryum borsigianum K. Koch. Although this was in a different genus, he should still have used the earlier epithet and failing to do so makes Wendland's own species name illegitimate.

The editor of the journal, Charles Lemaire, gave the etymology of the strange generic name as from *phoenix* (the date palm) and *phorion* (stolen), but tactfully left room for doubt as to the meaning of this: 'Il y a là une allusion dont l'auteur du genre *peut seul lever le voile*! Il se pourrait aussi que ce fût une allusion au pillage éhonté qui a eu lieu assez récemment des îles Séchelles(?)'. A footnote to Balfour's account (in Baker, 1877: 388) is less equivocal, and stated that the name was 'invented for the purpose of commemorating the disgraceful fact of a specimen of this Palm having been stolen from Kew by a foreign employé.' On these grounds *Phoenicophorium* is suppressed and Duncan's *Stevensonia* reinstated (the note is unattributed, and its robust defence of Kew's honour suggests Baker's hand.) Unfortunately botanical nomenclature does not allow Balfour (or Baker if it was his suggestion) to 'suppress' a validly published name, and as Wendland's name was earlier it has to stand! Wendland stated that the palm was introduced into cultivation by the firm of Ambroise Verschaffelt 'il y a huit ou neuf ans [i.e. around 1856/7]' directly from the Seychelles, but the Kew version of the story is different (Hooker, 1893) – according to the Curator John Smith the plant was sent to Kew by Duncan in 1855 and he set aside a plant to give to Wendland when he visited Kew in 1857. When they reached the 'nursery pits to show it to him, it was not to be found. This led to a strict enquiry, and it was found that it had been stolen by a German gardener then employed in the Gardens, and it afterwards appeared in a private garden in Berlin'. Such thefts were by no means unusual in the cut-throat business of nineteenth century horticulture.

Duncan was undoubtedly at the receiving end of academic snobbery, as demonstrated by his entry in the historical introduction to the *Flora* written by the arch-Kewite, and Hooker lackey, J.G. Baker, which consists of a meagre five lines – a reference to his *Catalogue* and the single sentence 'Duncan was the predecessor of Mr. Horne, in the curatorship of the Botanic Garden, at Pamplemousses, and died lately in Scotland.' He didn't even get poor Duncan's place of death right! By contrast, the Bohemian Bojer, a *bona fide* botanist, receives 28 lines in the same work, despite the fact that his *Hortus Mauritianus* is also little more than a list of names. Barriers of race were evidently more porous than those of the baize (or potting shed) door. However, there is perhaps more to it than this and if Duncan had been more assiduous in sending Hooker herbarium specimens (these are still the essential raw material of taxonomy) his contribution would have been more adequately recognised by botanists. Growing plants in gardens is simply not enough – even in places where hurricanes do not rage, plants in cultivation are more or less ephemeral, whereas those in herbaria are potentially immortal.

Nonetheless Duncan occupies a tiny niche in botanical literature, and Kew has made amends by including him in the official list of '*Authors of Plant Names*' (Brummitt & Powell, 1992). It is this list that gives the standard forms of those cryptic abbreviations that appear after Latin plant binomials. There are no fewer than seven botanical Duncans, but James is treated as the most senior (though chronologically he is not), requiring no qualifying initial when appearing after a plant name. Some of Duncan's names (even ones lacking descriptions) are included in *Index Kewensis*, where his *Catalogue* is cited as 'Cat. Hort. Maur.'. Somewhat surprisingly the *Catalogue* is not included in the (normally admirably thorough) standard work on botanical literature Stafleu & Cowan's '*Taxonomic Literature*' (TL2) – and so the title of the work has no official modern abbreviation. This is, perhaps, an indication of the rarity of Duncan's work in even well-stocked botanical libraries.

The following are Duncan's names:

Latania aurea Duncan, Cat. Hort. Maur. 56 (1863), *nom. nud.* (now = **Latania verschafeltii** Lem.).

Stevensonia Duncan, Cat. Hort. Maur. 87 (1863), *nom. nud.*

Stevensonia Duncan ex Balf. f. in Baker, Fl. Maur. 388 (1877) (now = **Phoenicophorium** H. Wendl.)

Stevensonia grandifolia Duncan, Cat. Hort. Maur. [Errata page] (1863) ['*grandiflora*' on p. 87], *nom. nud.*

Stevensonia grandifolia Duncan ex Balf. f. in Baker, Fl. Maur. 388 (1877) (now = **Phoenicophorium borsigianum** (K. Koch) Stuntz).

'*Stevensonia viridifolia* Duncan' mentioned as a name in a discussion, though not described or validly published, in an article by Berthold Seemann in the *Gardeners' Chronicle* 1870: 697 (1870) (now = **Verschaffeltia splendida** H. Wendl.).

REFERENCES

Baker, J.G. (1877). *Flora of Mauritius and the Seychelles*. London: L. Reeve & Co.

Bojer, W. (1837). *Hortus Mauritianus*. Maurice: Aimé Mamarot et Compagnie.

Duncan, J. (1863). *Catalogue of Plants in the Royal Botanical Garden Mauritius*. Mauritius: H. Plaideau.

Hooker, J.D. (1893). Stevensonia grandifolia. *Botanical Magazine* 119: t. 7277.

Wendland, H. (1865). De deux nouveaux genres de palmiers. *L'Illustration Horticole* 12: Misc. 5–6.

List of illustrations

Notes and Sources

Abbreviated names of sources are as follows:

BL British Library

DFA   Duncan Family Archives

DMB   Dictionary of Mauritian Biography

ODNB Oxford Dictionary of National Biography

KLA   Royal Botanic Gardens, Kew, Library and Archives

KEBC Royal Botanic Gardens, Kew, Economic Botany Collections

NAM   National Archives, Mauritius

PRO   Public Record Office (The National Archives, London)

Single name references are to sources listed in the Bibliography which follows. 'JD' refers to James Duncan.

2. Ile de France

1. For this introductory chapter, I have drawn generally on Addison and Hazareesingh.

2. Grove, p. 132. His *Green Imperialism* contains a very stimulating account of the importance of Mauritius in the emergence of environmentalism.

3. Rouillard and Guého, p.3. *Le Jardin des Pamplemousses, 1729-1979* is essential reading for anyone remotely interested in the history of the Botanic Garden at Pamplemousses.

4. Grove, p. 196

5. Ly-tio-fane, p. 8. Part of the first shipment of nutmegs that arrived in December 1753 was given to François-Etienne Le Juge, a plant lover who had started a model garden at Mongoust in Pamplemousses. Much later, this land, known as Le Petit Jardin, was linked to the Botanic Garden by the so-called Pont des Soupirs, or Bridge of Sighs. It was in other respects separated from the Garden by a river and was enclosed by the Flacq and Mapou roads. John Newman bought the land in 1829, built a house on it, and sold it on to the government in 1848. All this means that James Duncan's house was almost certainly on, or near, the site of the 1753 planting of nutmegs.

6. Louis Malleret, *Pierre Poivre, l'abbé Galloys et l'introduction d'espèces botaniques et d'oiseaux de Chine à l'Ile Maurice*, 1968, quoted by Rouillard and Guého pp. 21-22.

7. Nicolas Céré letter to Sonnerat, 1 August 1778, quoted by Ly-tio-fane p. 16.

8. Grove, p. 172

3. A British colony

1. O'Brian, pp. 308-9

2. Rouillard and Guého, p. 35

3. Rouillard and Guého, p. 35, quoting J.V. Thompson, *A catalogue of the exotic plants cultivated in Mauritius at the Botanic Garden*, 1816.

4. Rouillard and Guého, p. 36

5. Grant, chapter 29

6. *Kew Bulletin*, 1919, pp. 279-286

7. Rouillard and Guého, p. 38, quoting Surtees, Report of the Committee of Superintendance of the Royal Botanic Garden, 31 December 1844

8. John Newman to Colonial Secretary, 26 April 1848, NAM, RA 956

9. Dorr, p. 50

10. W. Bojer to Colonial Secretary, 27 February 1849, NAM, RA 1028

4. James Duncan – the early years

1. James seems to have cut himself off from his Aberdeenshire background. Yet his grandson George Duncan was to give *his* eldest son the name of Banchory in 1907.

2. DFA

3. RHS, *Handwriting Book of Under Gardeners and Labourers*. James Duncan was a not uncommon name. The India Office records within the British Library have a card index of Britons who spent time in India in the 18th and 19th centuries. There are cards for no fewer than twenty James Duncans.

4. Curiously, in the 1881 census, she is entered as being aged 46, fully five years older than her actual age at that time.

5. The Greys and the Hookers

1. Smith, p. 71, quoting J.M.Fewster, 'Prize money and the British Expedition to the West Indies 1793-4', *Journal of Imperial and Commonwealth History*, xii 1983, 1-28

2. Smith says that Eliza was born in Aix-en-Provence (p. 14); Foreman says she was born in a house near Montpellier (p. 266).

3. Allan, p. 68
4. McCracken, pp. 103-105
5. Allan, p. 148
6. Colquhoun pp. 156-8

6. Howick Hall
1. Smith, p. 138
2. House of Commons Research Paper 02/44, 11.7.02. Or only £4268 according to Economic History Services.
3. Information from Robert Jamieson
4. Howick Estate cash book, 1840-45
5. Pevsner, *Northumberland*, pp. 351-2
6. ODNB and letter from JD to Sir William Hooker, 29 November 1854, KA, DC LV 99. Incidentally, this Sir George Grey is not to be confused with the identically named Governor of New Zealand.
7. Hon. C. Grey, p. 419
8. *Howick Diary*
9. Howick Estate ledger 1846
10. Colquhoun, pp. 41-42
11. *Howick Diary*
12. Earl Grey, pp. 5-11, 37-41, 50, 54-7
13. ibid., p. 349
14. Earl Grey to Sir George Anderson, 29 May 1849, NAM, SA44 – No 82 – Fols 477-479

7. To Mauritius
1. Sir William Hooker to Sir F. Rogers, 18 March 1865, NAM, SA85 – No 74
2. Earl Grey to Sir William Hooker 4, 9, and 25 July 1849, KLA, DC 27, 204-7
3. Earl Grey to Sir William Hooker 21 December 1849, KLA, DC 33, 136
4. JD to Sir William Hooker 27 July 1849, KLA, DC LIV, 125. James never did get refunded the cost of his passage.
5. DMB
6. Earl Grey to Sir George Anderson 25 August 1849, NAM, SA44 – No 130 – Fols 775-777
7. Darwin, chap. 21. A slightly later European visitor to Mauritius was Charles Baudelaire, who spent two weeks there in September 1841. He described the

island in a sonnet as the 'pays parfumé que le soleil caresse,' and imagined palm trees raining down idleness on the writer's eyes.

8. Sadie, vol. 3, p. 276

8. Safe arrival

1. Rouillard p.17, quoting C. Cunningham, Report of the Committee of Council on the Botanical Gardens, 1848
2. Flemyng, p. 195
3. Addison and Hazareesingh p. 50
4. DFA

9. First reports

1. Earl Grey to Sir George Anderson, 24 April 1850, Earl Grey letters, Durham
2. JD to Colonial Secretary, 15 October 1850, NAM, RA 1084. The illustration of James's handwriting does not come from this letter – his spelling varied freely between 'honor' and 'honour'. The Colonial Secretary was the local official who headed the day to day functions of colonial government and acted as deputy to the Governor. Confusingly, the title was often applied also to the minister in the British government with responsibility for the colonies. In Earl Grey's time, the official title for this post was that of Secretary of State for War and the Colonies, though he described himself as Secretary of State for the Colonial Department.
3. JD to Earl Grey, 1 November 1850, PRO, CO 167/326. 'Malabars' were Indian labourers from Kerala.
4. JD to Sir William Hooker, 7 November 1850, KLA, DC LV, 85
5. KEBC, cat. no. 55073

10. 'This beautiful and fertile island'

1. Earl Grey, pp. 115-6
2. Brouard, p. 33 and Grove, pp. 378-9
3. Mouat, pp. 23-24. As a doctor, Mouat would have had formal training in botany.
4. JD to Colonial Secretary, 8 November 1851, NAM, RA 1131
5. JD to Colonial Secretary, 30 December 1851, NAM, RA 1131
6. NAM, Report of the Finance Committee no. 306, 24 January 1852

11. Collecting plants

1. JD to Sir William Hooker, 27 March 1852, KLA, DC LV, 87
2. JD to Sir William Hooker, 7 April 1852, KLA, DC LV, 88, 89

interchange of this nature are the measure of the usefulness of these Establishments; and it is only needful to refer to the eminent services rendered by the Botanic Gardens of Ceylon, Calcutta, Victoria, Jamaica and the Mauritius, as cases in point.'

5. Report of civil service commissioners, KLA, DC LVI, 104

6. Colonial Secretary to JD, 22 September 1860, KLA, DC LVI, 103

7. JD to Colonial Secretary, 22 September 1860, KLA, DC LVI, 109

8. JD to Sir William Hooker, November 1860, KLA, DC LVI, 101

9. JD to Colonial Secretary, 24 November 1860, NAM, RA1568

10. An unused and decaying house answering to this description can be seen today among other buildings at the south-east corner of the Garden.

11. Colonial Secretary to JD, 28 February, KLA, DC LVI, 106

12. JD to John Smith, 28 February 1861, KLA, KCL/1 Various Collectors 1791-1865, folio 148

13. John Ferguson to JD, 14 December 1860, DFA. It is possible that Ferguson was a relative by marriage, as he ends the letter by asking James to pass on 'my fondest love' to his brother-in-law and family.

14. Sir William was to die in 1865, aged 80.

15. The Duke of Newcastle was Secretary of State for the Colonies from 1859 to 1864.

16. JD to Sir William Hooker, 4 January 1862, KLA. In the same letter, James reported that he had sent boxes of fibres and spices to London for the International Exhibition of that year. He was to receive a medal for these.

16. *Catalogue of Plants*

1. JD to Colonial Secretary, 21 September 1960, NAM, RA 1568

2. Brouard, pp. 31-32. Brouard claimed that James's catalogue was written 'with Bojer's cooperation', but this seems most unlikely given that James Duncan did not start serious work on the catalogue until John Horne arrived at the end of 1861, while Bojer had died in 1856.

3. JD to Sir William Hooker, KLA, DC LVI, 108

4. Brouard, p. 40

5. The booklet was and is what might be called a rare work. By the end of 1865, 45 copies had been given away, and 33 copies had been sold, at a price of 4 shillings each. KLA, Misc Rep: Maur Bot Gdn 1865-1893, 3

6. Rouillard and Guého, pp. 40-41

7. Allan, p. 182

8. 'These days one has to be a high ranking civil servant to aspire to become owner of a *Bougainvillea splendens.' Le Cernéen*, 9 June 1862, quoted by Rouillard and Guého, pp. 40-41

9. 'We appreciate that the reign of the cinnamon trees is over, and that the garden's mango trees have been dethroned by species introduced more recently.'

10. Bernardin de Saint-Pierre, p. 133. 'The gift of a useful plant seems to me to be more precious than the discovery of a gold mine and a monument more lasting than a pyramid.'

11. Rouillard and Guého, pp. 9-10

17. Departure

1. Dr Joseph D. Hooker to JD, 4 August 1863, DFA. *Acrostichum* and *Lycopodium* are ferns. Dracaenas are now popular indoor plants. The fibres of *Dracaena macrophylla* are KEBC catalogue no. 36815. Gustav Mann (1836-1916) was a collector on the Niger Expedition 1859-62 before going to India.

2. JD to Joseph Hooker, 5 October 1863, KLA, DC 218, 72-73. Cinchona plants were needed for the production of quinine, at that time the only effective treatment of malaria. Along with rubber, cinchona seeds were one of the two great introductions from South America to Kew in the 19th century, for onward transmission to countries in Asia. Cinchona plantations had been started in India and Ceylon in 1860 and by 1863 quinine was available in India at low prices. (Allan p. 206)

3. Colonial Secretary to JD, 24 February 1864, NAM, RA 1742

4. DFA

5. JD to Colonial Secretary, 22 February 1864, NAM

6. JD to Colonial Secretary, 13 March 1864, NAM

7. Swinburne Ward, Civil Commissioner, Seychelles, to Colonial Secretary, 17 March 1864, NAM

8. Sir Henry Barkly to the Duke of Newcastle, 15 March 1864, NAM, SD 70 – No 80. This letter was misinterpreted by McCracken (*Gardens of Empire*, p. 48), when he wrote, 'When the great governor-botanist Henry Barkly arrived in the colony in 1863 he rated Pamplemousses a "wilderness".' He might well have done so, given the damage caused by the great storm of 1861, but in fact Barkly was making precisely the opposite point.

9. Sir William Hooker to Sir F. Rogers, 18 March 1865, NAM, SA 85 – No 74. Hooker's views on the appropriate training for a botanist are a little ironic given that he never went to university himself, but obtained all his botanical skills and knowledge through practical experience. It is interesting that JD was sent to see

the great Dr Lindley before being appointed to the Mauritian post – there is no other documentary evidence of this.

10. Sir Henry Barkly to Mr Cardwell, 5 May 1865, KLA, MR, Maur. Bot. Gdn 1860-1919, 33

11. DMB

18. 'A favourite resort'

1. Pike, pp. 72-79

2. Henry Noltie gives an account of the naming of this palm in his *A Botanist's Comments*.

3. Owadally, p. 14

19. Epilogue

1. DFA

2. JD to Sir William Hooker, 4 March 1861, KLA

3. DFA

4. McCracken, chapter 6. He also refers specifically to Pamplemousses, but this is in relation to John Newman, and James went out of his way to criticise Newman's behaviour.

5. John Corbett, whose first job was that of clerk in the colonial secretary's office in Port Louis, later became a nurseryman. The files in the National Archives of Mauritius for 1864 contain for the first time a listing of some of the recipients of plants from the Garden. One of the largest recipients was J.C. Duncan. He acquired 50 plants on 23rd May, 150 on 29th September, 100 on 6th October, 100 more on 8th October, and 120 on 10th October. His father had already left Mauritius by this time.

6. DMB

7. The house no longer exists, victim of redevelopment.

8. Perhaps there is a connection between this Scott and the Alexander Scott who had married James Duncan's stepsister, and who had registered William Duncan's death in 1861.

9. *Kew Bulletin*, 1894, p.136

10. DFA

BIBLIOGRAPHY

Published sources (books)

Addison, J. and Hazareesingh, K., *A New History of Mauritius*. Rose-Hill, Mauritius: Editions de l'Océan Indien, 1993

Allaby, Michael, *Oxford Dictionary of Plant Sciences*. Oxford: Oxford University Press, 2004

Allan, Mea, *The Hookers of Kew*. London: Michael Joseph, 1967

Anderson, R.D., *Education and Opportunity in Victorian Scotland*. Edinburgh: Edinburgh University Press, 1983

Baker, J.G., *Flora of Mauritius and the Seychelles*. London: Reeve, 1877

Barnwell, P.J. and Toussaint, A., *A short History of Mauritius*. London: Longmans, Green & Co., 1949

Beaton, Rev Patrick, *Creoles and Coolies; or, five years in Mauritius*. London: James Nisbet & Co, 1859

Bennett, P.R., *Mauritius [volume 140, World Bibliographical Series]*. Oxford: Clio Press, 1992

Benoît, Norbert, *Le Théâtre de Port Louis*. Port Louis: Vizavi, 1994

Bernardin de Saint-Pierre, Jacques-Henri, *Journey to Mauritius*, trs by Jason Wilson. Oxford: Signal Books, 2002

Bernardin de Saint-Pierre, Jacques-Henri, *Paul et Virginie*. Paris, 1788

Blunt, Wilfrid, *The Art of Botanical Illustration*. London: Collins, 1950

Bojer, W., *Hortus Mauritianus, ou enumeration des plantes exotiques et indigènes qui croissent à l'ile Maurice*. Port Louis,1837

Britten, J. and Boulger, G.S., *A biographical index of deceased British and Irish botanists*. London, 1931

Brouard, N. R., *A history of woods and forests in Mauritius*. Port Louis, 1963

Carter, Ian, *Farm life in north-east Scotland 1840-1914*. Edinburgh: John Donald, 1979

le Clézio, J.M.G.: *Voyage à Rodrigues*. Paris: Gallimard, 1986

Colquhoun, Kate, *A thing in disguise*. London: Fourth Estate, 2003

Darwin, Charles, *The Voyage of the Beagle*. London, 1839

Defoe, Daniel, *Robinson Crusoe*. London, 1719

Desmond, R., *Dictionary of British and Irish botanists and horticulturalists*. Basingstoke: Taylor & Francis, 1994

Dorr, L.J., *Plant Collectors in Madagascar and the Comoro Islands*. Kew: Royal Botanic Garden, 1997

Duncan, James, *Catalogue of plants in the Royal Botanical Garden, Mauritius*. Port Louis, 1863

Durrell, Gerald, *Golden bats and pink pigeons*. London: Collins, 1977

Ellis, Revd William, *Three visits to Madagascar during the years 1853-1854-1856*. London: John Murray, 1858

Flemyng, Rev. Francis P., *Mauritius; or The Isle of France: being an account of the island, its history, geography, products, and inhabitants*. London: Society for promoting Christian Knowledge, 1862

Fraser, W.Hamish & Lee, Clive H., *Aberdeen 1800-2000 a new history*. East Linton: Tuckwell Press, 2000

Gilbert, Lionel, *The Royal Botanic Gardens, Sydney*. Melbourne: Oxford University Press, 1986

Grant, Elizabeth, *Memoirs of a Highland lady*. Edinburgh: Canongate, 1988

Grey, Earl, The colonial policy of Lord John Russell's administration, 2 vols. London: Richard Bentley, 1853

Grey, Hon. C., *Some account of the life and opinions of Charles, Earl Grey*. London: Richard Bentley, 1861

Grove, Richard H., *Green Imperialism*. Cambridge: Cambridge University Press, 1995

Hart, W. Edward, *Le Jardin Botanique des Pamplemousses*. Port Louis: Imprimerie du Gouvernement, 1916

Hilton, Boyd, *A Mad, Bad, and Dangerous People? England 1783-1846*. Oxford: Oxford University Press, 2006

Hobhouse, Henry, *Seeds of Change*. London: Sidgwick & Jackson , 1985

Hollingworth, Derek, *They came to Mauritius*. Nairobi: OUP, 1965

Loudon, J.C., *An Encyclopaedia of Gardening*. London: Longman etc., 1835

Ly-Tio-Fane, M., *Mauritius and the spice trade – The odyssey of Pierre Poivre*. Port Louis: Esclapon Ltd., 1958

Matthew, H.C.G. & Harrison, Brian, ed., *Oxford Dictionary of National Biography*. Oxford: Oxford University Press, 2004

McCracken, D.P., *Gardens of Empire*. Leicester: Leicester University Press, 1997

Milbert, Jacques, *Voyage pittoresque à l'Ile de France*. Paris: A. Nepveu, 1812

Milton, Giles, *Nathaniel's nutmeg*. London: Hodder & Stoughton, 1999

Mouat, Frederic J., *Rough notes of a trip to Reunion, Mauritius and Ceylon*. Calcutta, 1852

Mueller, Ferdinand von, *Regardfully yours*, ed. R.W.Horne, 3 vols. Bern: Peter Lang, 1998, 2002, 2006

Noltie, H.J., *Indian Botanical Drawings 1793-1868*. Edinburgh: Royal Botanic Garden, 1999

O'Brian, Patrick, *Mauritius Command*. London: Collins, 1977

Owadally, A.W., *Sir Seewoosagur Ramgoolam Botanic Garden*. Mauritius, 2003

Pevsner, N, & Richmond, I, *Northumberland*. Harmondsworth: Penguin, 1992

Pevsner, N, *South and west Somerset*. Harmondsworth: Penguin, 1958

Pfeiffer, Ida, *Ida Pfeiffer's Last Travels*, trs by H.W. Dulcken, London: Routledge, 1861

Pike, Nicolas C., *Sub-tropical Rambles in the Land of the Aphanapteryx*. London: Sampson Low, Marston, Low, & Searle, 1873

Rivière, Lindsay, *Historical Dictionary of Mauritius*. Metuchen, N.J.: The Scarecrow Press, 1982

Rouillard, Guy, *Obelisque Liénard*, 150th anniversary commemoration. Port Louis: Royal Society of Arts and Sciences of Mauritius, 1979

Rouillard, Guy and Guého, J., *Le Jardin des Pamplemousses, 1729-1979*. Mauritius, 1983

Ryan, Vincent W., Bishop of Mauritius, *Mauritius and Madagascar: Journals of an eight years' residence*. London: Seeley, Jackson, and Halliday, 1864

Sadie, Stanley, ed., *The New Grove Dictionary of Opera*, 4 vols. London: Macmillan, 1992

Smith, E. A., *Lord Grey 1764-1845*. Oxford: O.U.P., 1990

Toussaint, A., ed., *Dictionary of Mauritian Biography*, 5 vols. Port Louis, 1941-84

Toussaint, A. & Adolphe, H., ed., *Bibliography of Mauritius 1502-1954*. Government of Mauritius, 1956

Published sources (articles in periodicals)

Botanical Magazine, 1 February 1893, t. 7277, J.D. Hooker, 'Stevensonia grandifolia'

Le Cernéen

26 April 1851

8 June 1862

9 June 1862

23 December 1863

Journal of Imperial and Commonwealth History, xii, 1983, pp 1-28, J.M. Fewster, 'Prize money and the British expedition to the West Indies'

Annals of Botany, xvi, 1902, J.D. Hooker, 'A sketch of the life and labours of Sir William Jackson Hooker'

Kew Bulletin

1894, p. 136, 'Drawings of Mauritius plants'

1919, pp. 279-286, 'The Botanic Garden of Pamplemousses', translated and abridged by F.R. Durham from W. Edward Hart's *Le Jardin Botanique des Pamplemousses*

Unpublished sources

British Library

Duncan Family Archives

University Library, Durham

Earl Grey letters GRE/B75/5A and 5B

Howick Diary

Howick Estate cash book, 1840-45

Howick Estate ledger, 1846

The National Archives, London

P.R.O. CO

National Archives, Mauritius

'Blue Book', Civil Establishment 1863

'Group R. Royal Botanic Garden Department', Secretariat Records 1811-80

Royal Botanic Gardens, Kew Library & Archives

Director's Correspondence

Various Collectors

Miscellaneous Reports:

Mauritius Miscellaneous 1849-1913

Mauritius Botanic Garden 1860-1919

Mauritius Botanic Garden 1865-1893

Royal Botanic Gardens, Kew

Economic Botany Collections

Royal Horticultural Society

Handwriting Book of Under Gardeners and Labourers

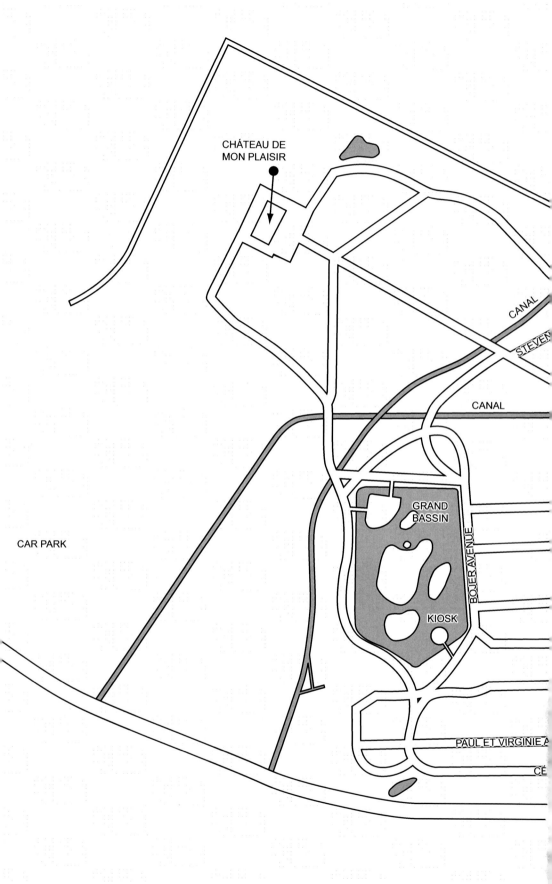

CHÂTEAU DE
MON PLAISIR

CANAL

STEVEN

CANAL

GRAND
BASSIN

CAR PARK

BOJER AVENUE

KIOSK

PAUL ET VIRGINIE A

CÉ